W9-DID-964

Where do I go
to get A LIFE?

Christmas 1995

for Alex

*because
you're already
there.*

Love, Mom

A GUIDE to
getting a grip on
your future.

Where do I go to get A LIFE?

Nicholas
COMNINELLIS

MULTNOMAH BOOKS · SISTERS, OREGON

WHERE DO I GO TO GET A LIFE?

published by Multnomah Books
a part of the Questar publishing family

© 1995 by Nicholas Comninellis, M.D.

International Standard Book Number: 0-88070-732-1

Edited by Stephen T. Barclift

Printed in the United States of America

Most Scripture quotations are from:
The Holy Bible, New International Version (NIV)
© 1973, 1984 by International Bible Society,
used by permission of Zondervan Publishing House

Also quoted:
The King James Version (KJV)

ALL RIGHTS RESERVED
No part of this publication may be reproduced, stored in a retrieval system,
or transmitted, in any form or by any means—electronic, mechanical,
photocopying, recording, or otherwise—without prior written permission.

For information:
Questar Publishers, Inc.
Post Office Box 1720
Sisters, Oregon 97759

95 96 97 98 99 00 01 02 — 10 9 8 7 6 5 4 3 2 1

ACKNOWLEDGEMENTS

I am grateful to the many people who helped with this book: Marian Flandrick Bray, Steve Brown, Paula Champ, Nathan Corbit, Curtis and Betty Dixon, Mark and Susan Hatfield, Dan Hickey, Paul Lively, Tim Lubinus, Bethany Mannor, Ron Reagan, and Cheryl Sander.

Also appreciated are the members of the Christian Medical/ Dental Society at the University of Missouri–Kansas City; the youth of Northside Community Church of Harare, Zimbabwe; and the saints of Liberty Christian Fellowship in Liberty, Missouri. They all patiently listened to and tested many ideas presented in these pages.

ACKNOWLEDGMENTS

CONTENTS

Life is like a journey each of us takes. We begin it holding our parents' hands. Gradually we learn about the world, begin to make our own decisions, chart our own course, and begin to run—albeit stumbling at times. We meet others along the way and form relationships as we travel.

But with seemingly unlimited potential destinations, where will this journey take us? What decisions must be made as we sojourn, and how should we go about making them? You may be about to embark on a college career and need to decide which school to attend, or in which area to study. Or, you may have completed a college education and now are confronted with job- or marriage-related decisions. Perhaps you are simply a young adult who feels you are drifting aimlessly through life, unsure the choices you make are wise ones. This book is for you.

Where Do I Go To Get A Life? presents a fresh perspective on decision-making. It provides the tools you need to make any decision, big or small. Taking an honest look at how we make decisions and use our lives demands courage. The implications can be far-reaching. But each of us can have a renewed hope and a fresh start, regardless of what road we have traveled before!

CHAPTER ONE

We Must Decide!

T he arrival of crisp fall weather brought many people to the Family Health Center where I worked as a resident physician in Fort Worth, Texas. In the treatment room, I'd just finished talking with a young pregnant woman about what to expect when she went into labor. As I said good-bye to her, the receptionist led in a desperate-looking man. "I have terrible chest pain," he managed to say. His face was tense. Gail, a nurse, attached him to the heart monitor and started an intravenous infusion. The man looked up at me and clutched my arm. He was sweating; his breathing was fast and shallow.

Soon, he lapsed into unconsciousness. "His blood pressure's falling!" Gail announced, looking up from the blood pressure cuff. A moment later the monitor showed a steady line—his heart had stopped beating. I grabbed the electric defibrillating paddles on the emergency cart and pushed them firmly against his chest. "Everyone stand back!" I shouted. I pressed the red buttons. With the electric jolt, his entire body jerked and his heart began to beat again. Relief poured over me. After a few moments he regained consciousness and looked up at me with an inquisitive smile. "What happened?" he ventured. Soon an emergency team arrived to take him to the hospital next door.

After a break to change my sweat-soaked shirt, I continued seeing patients. My next patient had smashed his thumb with a hammer. He'd broken no bones but had badly bruised the thumb. I quickly applied a splint, feeling like a fireman, putting out one fire after another.

As I opened the next examining door, a young man named Pete sat on the table. He was an athletic-looking fellow about twenty-two years old. I had seen him several times when he was younger. "How have you been, Pete?" I asked, shaking his hand.

"Doctor Nicholas, I'm about to graduate from college."

"Oh? Then this must be an exciting time for you," I replied. "How do you feel about it?"

"Well, I'm a little anxious. I need to make some big decisions about my life. I know you've made some good ones to get where you are now. I thought maybe you could help me."

I looked at him with surprise. This wasn't the type of request I usually received in the office. I reached for a chair. "What sort of decisions?"

"First, there's Heather. She and I have been dating for two years. I have strong feelings for her. We're thinking about getting married but she has another year of school to go."

"Are you sure she's the right one?" I asked.

Pete squirmed. "No, not one hundred percent sure. I'd like to have more time to decide."

"So what's the hurry?"

"For one thing, I've been offered a chance to teach biology at Sycamore High School. But that would mean moving to Clayton, eighty miles away from Heather. My degree is in biology and I'd like to teach. Teaching jobs are scarce, and I'm fortunate to have an offer."

"And that would make it hard to be with Heather," I said.

"Exactly. But that's not all. I'm interested in becoming a veterinarian. I think I have the grades to get into vet school here..." He stood and began to walk around the little room. "But if I apply, I can't begin my teaching job. The school wants a three-year contract."

"How long do you have to decide?"

"I've got just three weeks until the veterinary application deadline. To make things even more complicated, I'm broke. I really can't afford to go to graduate school *or* get married, the way things are now."

"Could you get a student loan or a scholarship?"

"Maybe. But I really don't want to go into debt. I talked to the Army recruiter at school yesterday. They would finance my education but then I would owe the Army several years." He looked out the window toward the parking lot and breathed a sigh. "I guess I really don't know what to do with my life."

We talked for another ten minutes about various options available to Pete. I encouraged him to get some advice from a career counselor. We agreed to meet together again in a week and Pete left.

On my way to lunch, I decided to stop by the intensive care unit and see the man with chest pain. I walked in and found him lying on his bed with anxious eyes. "Mr. Morgan," I said softly, "how are you feeling?"

"Like I fell down a flight of stairs. This is really scary."

"We're glad you have done so well," I said, trying to sound comforting. "Has your family come to see you yet?"

"The nurse called my wife...Doctor, I almost died today," he said with intensity, his voice close to breaking. "I've been lying here thinking about what I've done with my life—the decisions I've made. Life is really short; I've got to decide where to go from here." He glanced up with an expression of relief. "Here's my wife now!"

A very concerned lady appeared at the door. She was wearing a workout suit, as if she'd just come from a gym. She gave her husband a kiss, and I said good-bye to them both.

As I ate lunch, I wondered about Pete, my student friend. Had I been helpful to him? I also thought about Mr. Morgan's desire to redirect his life. What would he choose to do? My thoughts turned to my own struggles with decision-making. Even in college, I had been interested in working overseas. At the moment, I was considering going to war-torn Angola to work with a medical team. This wasn't an easy decision to make. Neither was Pete's! His career and marriage plans had reached a crossroads. Which way would he go? What should I say when I met with him next time? I pulled out a notebook and wrote, "Wanted: a wonderful life."

A WONDERFUL LIFE

We all want to have a wonderful life. We want to be successful, rewarded for our work, and to feel like what we are doing is worthwhile in the long run. We don't want to waste our time. These are good objectives! But each of us must choose how to live.

The quality of our lives depends greatly upon our decisions. And we are responsible for the choices we make.

At various times we're all in Pete's position. On the most superficial level, we ask questions about daily living: *Should I wash the car today? Can I afford to be a little late for work today? What shall I fix for supper?* On a deeper level, we decide what to study, whom to marry, where to live, with whom to be friends, and what attitudes to develop. The issue isn't simply deciding which career to pursue, as some think. We need to consider *all* important aspects of our lives. This can lead to tough, even philosophical, questions. J. Grant Howard, a seminary professor, put decision-making in perspective when he wrote:

> If life can be viewed as a battle, then here is the latest and most appropriate communiqué: We are completely surrounded and totally outnumbered. That is a realistic progress report from the weary foot soldiers on the front lines of life. Surrounded? Outnumbered? By what?
>
> Options! In the battle of life we are up against options. Everywhere we turn there are choices to be made. Obligations that pressure us. Opportunities that entice us. We are bombarded with places to go, overrun with people to meet, pinned down with things to buy, fatigued with mail to read. We are being inundated on all sides by powerful forces that clamor for our time, talents, money, influence, wisdom. There is also a psychological aspect to this campaign: We are infiltrated by feelings of guilt because we cannot possibly respond to all the options.

At times we are so pummeled with options that we contemplate surrender. We look in vain for a white flag to wave. Gradually we realize that we are under siege and that the siege lasts a lifetime. We can't surrender. We can't escape. We just keep on fighting. And the fight is carried on by making decisions. Some decisions involve only a minor skirmish; others are major. When we make the right choice, we win. If it's the wrong choice, we lose. There are no cease-fires, and tomorrow there will be more skirmishes.[1]

Time is a resource; we only have a limited amount of it. There are about twenty-five thousand days in the average lifetime. So how can we best use the time allotted to us? What decisions will we make? What should we do with our lives? All of us have thoughts like these at some time or another.

A scene from the wartime movie *The Bridge Over the River Kwai* illustrates this point. Between Burma and Thailand, cutting through deep forest, ran a great river. Very early one morning during World War II, a British commander and his benevolent captor, a Japanese officer, stood together on a bridge. For months the British prisoners of war had worked to construct this bridge in the jungle. Now the bridge was finished, and it was time to move on to another project. As the two men looked downriver, the British commander spoke to the Japanese officer about his life.

I've been thinking. Tomorrow it will be twenty-eight years to the day that I've been in the service. Twenty-eight years in peace and war. I don't suppose I've been at home more than ten months in all that time. Still, it's been a good life. I wouldn't have had it any other way. But there are times when

suddenly you realize you are nearer the end than the begin-
ning. And you wonder, you ask yourself what the sum total
of your life represents—what difference your being there at
any one time made, if any? Or if you made any difference at
all really, particularly in comparison to other men's careers? I
don't know if that kind of thinking is very healthy, but I have
to admit I have had some thoughts on those lines from time
to time.[2]

The commander realized he wouldn't live forever. He was
looking at his life and wondering if what he had done was worthwhile. Had he been a success? Had he put his effort into the right
areas? Had he made good decisions? What had he done with his
life? That same day, this commander was killed by his enemies.
Before our lives end, and better yet, before we go any further, let's
take a careful look at what *we* will decide to do with our lives.

BAD DECISIONS

I doubt very many of us deliberately set out to make trouble
for ourselves. Unfortunately, though, in spite of our good inten-
tions, many people make poor choices and pay a bitter price. Let's
look at some examples.

• One young man who blew it big time was Amnon. He was
a son of King David in ancient Israel (2 Samuel 13). Of course, as
a prince he was a very privileged person! But he had a weakness:
Amnon lusted for his half-sister, Tamar. He became so enamored
with her that he made himself sick. So he devised a plan. He
stayed in bed and asked her to come and make a meal for him.
When they were alone, he grabbed Tamar and forced her into bed

with him. She resisted, telling Amnon that what he wanted to do was wicked and foolish. But the prince was stronger, and he raped her.

Tamar was disgraced. She wept long and hard. Amnon threw her out of his room. In fact, his heart had changed completely. Now he hated her! It wasn't long before Tamar's brother Absalom heard what had happened. He was furious! Two years later he had his revenge—he had Amnon killed. Amnon made some bad decisions. He paid for them with his life!

• Phillip had a similar problem. He was twenty-three and worked in construction. I first met Phillip when he brought his father, Jim, to see me at the clinic. Jim had been a heavy drinker for years. Now he was suffering from liver failure. Jim's skin was deep yellow and he had a very large, fluid-filled abdomen. I cared for Jim in the hospital several times, but he finally died from complications of his drinking. I grieved Jim's death with Phillip and Phillip's young wife. It had been terrible to watch Jim go downhill day after day.

Six months later, Phillip and his wife came to see me. This time she had brought *him*. Phillip was drinking! I knew he was at risk for developing alcoholism because of his family background. Still, after witnessing the slow, painful death of his father, it was hard for me to believe Phillip would go the same way. We talked about rehabilitation, but he wasn't interested. We discussed the effect of alcohol on his family, finances, and physical health. Phillip's wife begged him to stop, but to all this he replied, "I can handle my drink."

A month later, Phillip was coming home from a party, drunk. He drove his car into a bridge pillar and was killed. He had been wrong about his ability to deal with alcohol. Like Amnon, he paid for his mistakes with his life. And Phillip's wife and children are still paying, with their grief and sorrow.

• Tommy and Kate had come to college with high expectations for the future. Tommy dreamed of a career in automobile design; Kate had her heart set on drama and modeling. The two of them met in the first week of fall classes, and it was "love at first sight." Tommy's heart pounded in his chest whenever Kate took his hand. He'd never experienced a relationship like this before! Kate was smitten by Tommy's good looks. She never thought someone so attractive could be interested in her.

A few weeks later, Tommy took Kate for a long walk through a park. He took both her hands, looked her straight in the eyes, and said, "Kate, will you marry me?" It took her only two seconds to respond. "Yes!" she said with glee.

Things moved even faster after this. The following weekend, Tommy went to meet Kate's parents to tell them the news. Wedding plans dominated their relationship for the next two months, and the ceremony was held during Christmas break. After a quick honeymoon in the mountains, Tommy and Kate were both back in classes.

Things went well enough for about three months. But then Kate began to have doubts. "You know, Tommy, this is really a big change for me. I want to spend more time with my girlfriends, and go out for the volleyball team. But you want me home every evening. I used to have enough money to buy clothes, but since we married, my parents say I'm on my own—and you and I don't have a penny. I want to finish school, but one of us is going to have to get a full-time job!"

Tommy was defensive. "Well, you're not the only one who is unhappy! I don't have time to study to get into my career track, let alone time to see my friends. I don't think I really know you after all. You're not the sweet girl I met six months ago; you were just acting that way to please me." He paused and sat down on the bed. "And I'm not the strong, shining knight you thought I was..." Tommy took in a long breath. "Maybe we shouldn't have decided to marry so soon..."

BETTER DECISIONS

Fortunately, poor decision-making doesn't need to be a permanent quality. Let's look at some people who made better choices about how to live.

• Matt Condon and I grew up near one another and went to high school together. We competed on the same sports teams, and often over the same girl's affections! We usually lost at both of these endeavors, but ended up winning each other's friendship. As I got to know him, I learned that Matt's father was an alcoholic, and that Matt's entire family was involved in an intervention and recovery program.

In high school Matt had a little trouble with drinking himself, but he managed to keep it under control. The problem really hit hard after he was married, had children, and was the pastor of a large church near Seattle. Matt went in and out of sobriety over a several-year-long period, condemning himself and often considering suicide. The temptation to hide or deny his alcoholism was great, for Matt knew he could lose his family, ministry, and income if the problem became known publicly. Yet he also knew that if he didn't confront the problem, it would eventually kill him, as it had his father.

One Sunday morning, Matt boldly stood before his congregation. "All of you have shown remarkable trust in me as a spiritual leader. One of the things I have emphasized is our need to confront our problems, confess our sins, and help one another. Today it's my turn to live out what I've been saying. I'm risking much to tell you this, but I have no other choice. I am an alcoholic, my problem has become uncontrollable, and I'm entering a treatment program tomorrow."

Instead of rejecting Matt, the people of his church surrounded him and his family with love and affection like Matt had never experienced before. After a year of rehabilitation, he returned to his ministry full-time. "But if I hadn't decided to confront my drinking," Matt declares, "I'd probably be dead today."

• Barry Borror is another man who is right on target. He began early in high school to think about what he wanted to do after graduation. Barry wrote letters to different colleges and organizations asking for information. When he was a senior, he had an interview with the school career counselor.

Barry opened the door of the counselor's office. "Come in," said Mr. Goodwin, a tall, muscular man who frequently ran his fingers through thinning hair. "Well, Barry," the counselor said, "your time here is almost up. Have you thought about what you might want to do when you graduate?"

Barry laid his folder of information on the desk in front of the counselor. "Yes, I have. After I graduate, I will attend junior college for a year of liberal arts studies—a requirement for a degree from Moody Bible Institute. I've already been accepted. At Moody,

I will major in mission aviation technology, which includes learning to be a pilot and an aircraft mechanic. That will be a three-year course." Barry spoke confidently, and Mr. Goodwin rubbed his forehead in amazement.

He continued. "When I graduate from Moody, I plan to go on staff with Mission Aviation Fellowship. I'll live in a foreign country and fly pastors, doctors, and relief supplies to remote areas. I've been looking at some personnel requests for Central America. So I'm presently taking a Spanish course."

Mr. Goodwin shook his head in awe. "That's fantastic! You're the first student I have counseled this year who has a plan worked out. You've already set some career goals. Most people don't do that until years after they graduate, if ever!"

Barry not only had a clear plan, he carried it out, doing everything he planned. I was one of the doctors he flew to remote villages in Honduras years later. In Barry Borror we see an example of a person whose direction in life was clear.

• Kevin and Nancy had a much different courting experience from that of Tommy and Kate, discussed earlier. Kevin was from a very small town and Nancy was a city girl. Their religious backgrounds were starkly different, too. What they did have in common was chemistry lab as freshmen at the University of Missouri–Kansas City. The two got to know each other as they jointly fouled up experiments. After a couple of semesters of this, they discovered some personal chemistry brewing between *them*.

For the next three years, Kevin and Nancy were almost inseparable. But their relationship rarely consisted of fancy dates. Instead, they spent time helping each another study, rescuing struggling friends, and working out their sticky philosophical differences. Nancy remarked, "I knew our relationship was looking secure when we began purchasing one textbook to share between us." They finally officially became engaged, to the elation of their friends. But financial restrictions held off the wedding for yet another year.

My friends know I love to sing and play my instruments. So I've performed at many weddings. But unlike several of the questionable unions I had witnessed, Kevin and Nancy's relationship was not only heartfelt, it was developed and tested over thousands of real-life encounters. It's no wonder that today their marriage is one of the best I know!

THE PRESSURE IS ON!

These stories illustrate some of the impact decision-making skills can have on our lives. Many of us get so caught up in the excitement or pressures of life that we don't think about the future. Our next date, exam, or party seems to occupy our thoughts most, with little time or energy left for anything more important. Others of us recognize our need to decide what to do next with our lives, but shrink back for lack of confidence or fear of failure. We've been hurt, it seems, by our earlier decisions, so why take another risk? Or we think there is no way out of our predicaments, so we don't try.

We can't afford to be swept along from event to event or crisis to crisis. This won't take us where we need to go. Nor can we allow ourselves to be timid or fall victim to strategic paralysis. Instead, each of us must boldly decide how to live and begin to pursue our goals courageously.

TAKE ACTION!

1) What are some good decisions you have made? What are some bad ones? Make a list of each.

2) Who among your friends seems to know with certainty what he or she wants to do in life? Go interview that person. Ask your friend how he or she makes decisions.

3) Do you know someone who you feel tends to make bad decisions? Discreetly observe this person. Without being judgmental, can you determine what he or she may be doing wrong?

CHAPTER TWO

So What's the Problem?

Judy snuggled more deeply into the covers on her cozy bed. She enjoyed this moment just before falling asleep—thinking over what had happened during the day. She took a deep breath, sighed, and closed her eyes...

Suddenly, a loud pounding boomed at the door of her apartment. "Help, Judy! Help me!" yelled a voice from outside. Judy sprang out of bed and stumbled around her bedroom, looking for the light. "Should I call the police?" she said aloud. "What if it's a thief trying to trick me?"

Judy slid toward the front window and stealthily peered out at the porch. She could just make out a figure in the shadows. As her eyes adjusted to the light, the figure became more clear: Judy saw a woman with tattered hair and bright red stains on her torn clothing. Squinting, she focused on the visitor's face.

"Marsha!" Judy gasped. She scrambled for the door, thinking of how they had met at basketball tryouts as freshmen. Marsha had had many tough breaks since then. What could it be now?

With a tug, the door burst open and Marsha fell into Judy's arms. Her face was purple from bruises on both cheeks. Blood ran from her nose and she held her left forearm as if it were broken. "Marsha, who did this to you?" pleaded Judy.

"Gilbert," she said with a sob. "But he really didn't mean to!"

Judy looked surprised. "I thought you two were in love. What happened?"

"You don't know him very well," replied Marsha, drying her eyes as they sat down in the tiny kitchen. "Neither did I when I met him. But he was so attractive! He also has a lot of money. I thought I'd finally met the right guy. Then things began to change." She paused a moment and tears came to her eyes. "I discovered Gilbert had a terrible temper. If a car passed him on the highway, he'd curse and honk the horn. If I was ten minutes late for a date, he'd stomp around and slam the door.

"But tonight was the worst." Her voice grew more tense. "Gilbert said he wanted to meet my parents, but when I suggested we weren't ready for that step, he lost control. He shoved me to the floor and began throwing things at me—the plates, a chair, pictures off the walls, even the crystal glasses. They shattered when they hit me. When he reached for the carving knife, I bolted from the house and ran for my life!

"But Judy," she continued, "what hurts even more than the bruises is knowing I denied how bad his problem is, when it was obvious all along! I told myself it was God's will for us to be together, but I should have stopped seeing him long ago."

Judy rocked Marsha in her arms and tried to comfort her. "Things will get better. You'll meet someone else."

Marsha shrugged her shoulders. "I don't know. I've always had problems deciding on the right guys to date. I don't trust my judgment anymore. Judy, why do I have so much trouble making good choices?"

DECISIVE STRUGGLES

Situations like Marsha's are common, and they are disturbing. But some of us seem to make better decisions than others, avoiding costly consequences. Let's look at three common problems in decision-making:

1) *Uncertainty about God's guidance.* Marsha believed it was God's will for her to be with Gilbert but then reconsidered after her frightening experiences. Many people believe they have received signs from God indicating that they should take a particular action. But later, they begin to doubt and ask, "Was this really God's will for me?" or "Did I interpret his leading correctly?"

John was a friend of mine who believed it was God's will that he join the military. So he joined with confidence. A year later, he found himself stationed on the other side of the world. At first this seemed to be a good experience. Then John began to miss his friends. He also became frustrated with the regulations. John began to wonder if God really *had* called him into the military. Perhaps God really had wanted him to go into business with his father! Uncertainty stole his joy and sapped his energy.

2) *Focusing on the wrong mission or purpose.* Marsha wanted an attractive, wealthy man for her husband. She found out the hard way that this wasn't enough. Likewise, many of us set our sights on things we believe will satisfy us, only to later discover we were deceived. We find our decisions were based on a wrong set of values in the first place.

Jack, one of my best friends, thought life would be wonderful if he could just earn $100,000 a year. He started a roofing business, working full-time plus nights, weekends, and holidays.

When a big tornado hit, the demand for his repair work soared. In just five years Jack was earning the magic six figures he desired.

But Jack began to feel terribly alone. His wife, ignored for months at a time, eventually had had enough of his emotional absence and left him. Jack's employees, tired of his relentless demands, stopped talking with him. He hadn't even called his brother in two years, though they lived in the same town and had been close previously. Jack discovered almost too late that a good salary alone was the wrong mission for his life.

3) *Failure to think through the consequences of our decisions.* Just as Marsha chose to continue dating Gilbert in spite of his problem with anger, too often we rationalize that "Things will work out all right," and follow what seems to be the easiest path. And in the end, we suffer so very much for our lack of foresight!

Maria interviewed for a job on the other side of the United States. The salary and benefits were good, meeting her primary criteria. When the job was offered to her, she accepted it and moved away. Soon, however, Maria discovered she missed her family terribly. And she couldn't find a church that compared with the one back home. If that weren't bad enough, she found that the boys in her new city were nothing like the one she'd left behind. Maria hadn't thought about how her career decision would affect all her relationships.

CHANGING COURSE

Fortunately, we don't have to be trapped in these three areas where our decisions often break down. We can learn to recognize problems, make better choices, and improve the course of our lives. Chris provides a good example of this. He was a good student, when he put his mind to it, and graduated from high school ahead of the rest of his class. He wasn't sure what to do next, but somehow secured a management job—in a printing company—and bought a fast car, a 240Z. Soon, however, he had wrecked the car and the job became boring. So Chris bought a motorcycle and hit the road.

He traveled across several states, working as a laborer for petroleum companies. But when the motorcycle broke down in Louisiana, Chris decided to try out the Job Corps to learn welding or another trade. He headed for the Job Corps headquarters in Colorado, where he took entrance exams. When the results came in, the director confronted him. "Chris, your academic skills are excellent. We don't want you here. We'll send you to college." So, quite indirectly, Chris wound up in the classroom again. But he also had ample free time, so he took up the electric guitar.

After graduation, Chris returned home, working by day and playing in a rock 'n' roll band by night. It was a hard existence and Chris had a growing sense of dissatisfaction with it all. He looked carefully at where he was going in life and crafted a plan designed to turn his life around. Gradually he began to implement this plan. He dropped the band and with it the drinking, cigarettes, parties, and late nights that had come to characterize his life. He took up running and eating health food. Chris then gave up his depressing job and started his own business, in graphics design. Forever fearful of marriage, he switched gears in this too, and married the woman he'd dated for years. Chris found a level of companionship that he'd never before dreamed of.

By taking stock of his life, recognizing how to improve his decisions, and boldly putting his plans into practice, Chris became a happy, content, and directed person. And I should know; Chris is my brother.

OUR CHALLENGE

You may think that what was possible for my brother might not be possible for you. Is there really anything we can do to improve our decision-making skills? The answer is *yes*. Our confidence and actual ability to manage our lives can greatly improve. We don't have to remain caught in any of the three decision-making traps, even if we've been stuck in one or more for years. We don't have to second-guess God's will. Instead, we can clearly understand and have a heart's desire for our mission in life. And it's usually possible to weigh our options carefully before we decide on a specific plan.

First, we need to realize good decisions usually don't just happen. Decision-making is a skill to be learned, just like playing basketball, driving a car, or balancing a checkbook. Good decisions usually take research, concentration, and considerable time. We need to put forth effort in order to see good results.

Second, we must realize that how we reach decisions is a complex process. As we'll see in subsequent chapters of this book, good decisions are the result of trustworthy leadership, a correct mission, and wisdom. We can't very well talk about a specific choice without establishing and clarifying the basics first.

Are you willing to work hard? Are you willing to broaden your thinking? If so, then you have taken the first steps toward making better decisions!

TAKE ACTION!

1)   What sort of problems have you had in the way you go about making decisions? Write down three of them.

2)   What has helped you to make good decisions in the past? Share your secret with a friend.

PART ONE

OUR
LEADER:

Jesus Christ

CHAPTER THREE

Whom Will You Follow?

L aura was a freshman on the college campus. She was pretty and very social. In high school she had dated many boys but had strong ideas about her sexuality; she wanted to remain pure for that special man who would one day be her husband.

Laura looked forward to making new friends. Soon she met Allen in her English class. When he asked her out on a date two weeks later, she was thrilled!

That Friday evening, Allen picked up Laura at her dorm. She was sure they would have a good time. First they went to a Chinese restaurant and talked about sports. Allen told her he was trying out for football and had a sore back from working out with the team. From there they went to a movie at the student union. Laura saw several of her new friends. Her roommate, Paula, and her date were also there. Laura was happy she had shown up with such a good-looking guy.

While they were driving home, Allen asked Laura if she wanted to see where he lived. She was eager to please, and said yes. But she grew more hesitant. She didn't know him well. Allen had an apartment off campus. After showing Laura around his small place, he began to complain about his back aching. He lay down on the big couch in the living room. When she was close,

Allen pulled her down next to himself. He began to kiss her passionately, and to unbutton her blouse.

Laura tried to get up and shouted with anger, "You can't do this to me!" She began to rebutton her blouse.

"I just want to show you how much I like you," Allen said reassuringly. "Come on..." He began to move toward her again.

"Don't touch me!" Laura shouted. "I went out with you to be friends and have fun, not to go to bed with you!"

"Oh, come off it," said Allen, now angry himself. "All of us sleep with our dates. There's nothing wrong with a little love. If you don't go along, no one will ever go out with you."

"I don't care. I'm going to wait until I marry to have sex—with my *husband.*"

He laughed. "Where'd you come up with that idea? I just want to play, and you're missing out on all the fun!"

"I don't have to take this. I'm going home!" Laura ran out of the apartment and slammed the door. As she walked back to the dorm, she sobbed and prayed, "God, I feel so abused. Are all the guys here going to be like this? Please help me!"

It was late when Laura arrived at the dorm. She wanted to talk to her roommate, Paula. Laura was drying her tears as she walked into her room. It was dark but there was a little candle burning on her desk. She heard some stirring from her roommate's bed.

Then Paula spoke up. "Oh, Laura, could you wait outside until Drew leaves?"

Laura's mouth dropped open. Paula was in bed with her date! She turned and bolted from the room. Alone in the dorm study room, Laura sat crying and said through her tears, "I think it's right to wait until I'm married, but everyone else thinks they should have sex now. This is so hard to take! Allen probably will tell his friends, and no one will ever want to date me. And Paula will think I'm old-fashioned." She stopped sobbing and straightened up. "But I don't care what they think. I'm not going to give myself to just anyone! I don't want a broken heart, or AIDS, or to be pregnant before I'm ready. What I want to know is, where are people getting their crazy values?"

WE'RE SURROUNDED!

Each of us is profoundly influenced by those around us. Even people who consider themselves self-reliant and self-directed must admit this is true. But we get conflicting information about how to live. To make good decisions about our sexuality, or about anything else, we need to know whom we can trust for advice and guidance. Laura was listening to a far different message—spoken by Christian friends and people in her church—than were Allen or Paula.

Consider the situation of a friend of mine, Jo Anne. She recently graduated from high school. A short time after graduation, she met the man of her dreams and decided to marry him right away. Her father told Jo Anne she should wait to marry until she is older. But her friends were very excited for her and encouraged her to become engaged. Jo Anne's favorite teacher, who used to counsel me in high school, told her to hold out for a better guy. Her pastor told her it's all right to marry now as long as the man is a Christian. Jo Anne's brother, on the other hand, whose short-term marriage is breaking up, is still asking her to wait a while. I don't know what she will decide to do, but all these people are influencing Jo Anne's final decision about marriage.

Who are *you* listening to? Where can you get good advice? Look at some of the people who have an impact on your capacity to make good decisions:

- Parents
- Friends
- Professors
- Mass media practitioners: television, radio, book, and magazine producers
- Advertisers and salespeople
- Church leaders
- Employers
- Co-workers.

Consciously or not, all these people tell us how to live by promoting their own values. A value is a way of assigning worth. Some things are more important to us than others. For instance, people who strongly value human life often give money to help relieve hunger. Others, who highly value their appearance, put money into clothing and cosmetics. As we grow and learn, we assign value to almost everything. Our value system then becomes the "eyeglasses" through which we see the world, and the base from which we make decisions. Our decisions reveal our true values. So we must carefully screen just which values we will adopt for our own!

Values can vary greatly—just look at the concept "success" for example. Americans are very success-oriented. We speak about success in finances, marriage, business, and friendships. Seminars on success crop up everywhere on subjects as diverse as investing, management, advertising, and church growth.

People hold widely divergent ideas about success. The advertising industry tells us success is to own a certain make of car or brand of watch. Many business people define success by one's professional position and income. A popular image of success is a person with a high-paying job, a lovely spouse, happy and well-behaved children, time for hobbies, a house in the country, and perfect physical health. To others, success means freedom from responsibilities, time to travel, unrestricted enjoyment of life, and avoidance of relationships that require much commitment.

What is true success? Society offers us a smorgasbord of opinions. However, these often contradict one another, as we've just seen. What's more, what people think about success, sexuality, and hundreds of other matters changes over time. This creates more tension, and even confusion. We're surrounded by people clamoring for our attention and allegiance. Who should we trust to guide our decisions? Ourselves alone? Our friends or professors? Is there anyone who is *more* reliable?

WHAT IS THE TRUTH?

Deep within each of us is the desire for certainty, for *truth*, to guide our thoughts and actions. But "truth" is not simply an abstract concept. Truth is a *Person*—Jesus Christ.

Jesus did amazing things when he was on the earth. He healed the sick (Matthew 8:1-17) and miraculously fed the hungry (Matthew 14:13-21). The outcasts of society became some of his best friends, an extraordinary action for anyone of that time

(John 9:34-38). He even brought back to life some people who had died (Luke 7:11-17; John 11:1-44)! Jesus trained and transformed undisciplined men and women who literally changed the world.

But the most remarkable thing is not what Jesus did but who he is—God himself. Jesus calls himself the Light of the World (John 8:12, 12:35-36), and the Bread of Life (John 6:22-58). Not only has he spoken the truth, he is the truth. Jesus says, "I am the way and the truth and the life. No one comes to the Father except through me" (John 14:6). Jesus proved his profound words not only through his miracles, but by rising again to physical life after he was brutally executed (Matthew 28:6). Jesus is our best possible guide in life. Why? Because he has all the knowledge and power of God, and because he has experienced all the temptations, pains, and joys of being human.

So how can we discover what he says? The first place to look is the Bible. Written by God-inspired people who walked with Jesus and often died because of his message, it's the standard by which Christians should live (Psalms 119:11, 105). Hundreds of controversial subjects are addressed within its pages. Yet in spite of its diverse background, the Bible is consistent in content and message. It's much more than merely a collection of facts: The Bible is inspired by our God who cares for us and gives us hope in the midst of our problems (Romans 15:4)!

As we struggle to make good decisions, we don't have to give in to the influences of advertisers, politicians, professors, friends, or even our own prejudices and experiences. Jesus Christ came to earth to bring new life. He came to give us the direction and inner strength we need to live to our full potential. Jesus wants each of us to have such a life. He says, "I have come that they may have life, and have it to the full" (John 10:10). Peter and Paul, two of the first people to trust Jesus, lived radically transformed and inspired lives. The same life-changing Person is at work today. Through the Bible and the work of his Spirit, Jesus is still showing his followers a refreshing identity and fulfilling way of life.

CHANGING MAJORS

Let's take a look at how Christ impacted the life of a young man named Carl. He was a bright student who, while still in high school, decided to pursue a professional career. His father was behind him completely. Carl chose a college where he could study geology; he intended to land a job in oil exploration. He was confident this would enable him to advance to a high position and make a very good income. With this goal in mind, Carl studied hard and did well in school.

But in his sophomore year, something remarkable happened. Carl had never been very interested in spiritual things—at least not until he met Andrew, another sophomore. They played basketball together, and Andrew invited Carl to a weekend clinic sponsored by the local professional basketball team.

During the noon break, the aspiring athletes gathered in a circle outside as they ate and listened to Michael, the center for the city's pro team. Michael talked about his relationship with Jesus Christ. At first Carl was a little uncomfortable. But as Michael continued, Carl became curious about what this man was saying. When the session was over, Carl went right up to Michael and said he wanted to believe in Jesus, too. The two of them went to a nearby park bench and prayed together.

Carl's life began to change dramatically after that. He made more time for people. His face was brighter. He met with a group of Christians every week. His father noticed the difference when Carl came home for spring break. One day they were talking during breakfast.

"Carl, you seem different; I mean, happier. Do you have a new girlfriend?"

"No, Dad. But I am a different person now. I made some big decisions this term."

His father looked at him curiously. "What kind of decisions?"

"Dad, I've become a Christian. I believe in Jesus now."

His father looked puzzled. "But don't we all, son?"

"I don't mean just going to church—I mean a real commitment to him. I see Jesus working in my life and I want to follow him, no matter what." His father still had that puzzled look on his face, so Carl continued. "I have also decided to change my major."

His father's face changed from a look of curiosity to one of concern. "To what?"

"I've decided to become a social worker."

"A social worker!" Now his father's face was turning red. "Why on earth do you want to be a social worker?"

"The only real reason I went into geology was to make lots of money. God has shown me there are more important things in life than that."

"Like what?"

"People, Dad. I want to help people. That's more important. Social work will give me a way to do that."

"But how will you make enough money to enjoy life?"

"But Dad, that's not what really matters," Carl replied.

The two of them sat quietly together. It seemed like hours to Carl. Finally, his father looked at him and said, "You must be really serious about what you believe!"

Carl's decision to believe in and follow Jesus caused him to change much more than his career track. He, like his father, once had an intellectual understanding of Christianity. Now, however, Carl had gone much further. Jesus Christ became the center of his life. What is it about Jesus that can be so life-changing? What is his message? It can be summed up in two words: security and leadership.

OUR SECURITY: JESUS CHRIST

Jesus loves each one of us, regardless of how we feel about him in response. He isn't an impersonal force somewhere in the universe, or a distant historical figure. Jesus is more concerned for us today than we can imagine!

But if Jesus loves us so much, why don't more people feel that love? Often this is due to sin. Sin is the choice we make to ignore God and go our own way. It's the rejection of his love, inner healing, and leadership, and it puts us in a spiritual wasteland. We're all familiar with the dangers of physical disease. The Bible says sin is a *spiritual* disease and that we all suffer from it. It's a disease that has far greater consequences than cancer or a heart condition. It results in a spiritual death—separation from God forever (Romans 5:12, 6:23; Ephesians 2:1-3).

We're in a tragic condition, but God offers us a cure. When Jesus Christ was killed, he took upon himself the punishment we deserve for our sin. he was our substitute—our replacement—enabling us to get right in our relationship with God (1 Peter 1:18-21). Jesus didn't give up something superficial or replaceable to save us—like a car, fancy wardrobe, or CD collection that *we* might value. *Jesus loved us so much that he gave up his very life*, dying a terribly painful death. And all along he had the power to stop his own execution—but he died anyway. He did this to bridge the gap between us and God.

The good news is that we can receive new spiritual life by believing in Jesus Christ. This means believing in who Jesus is (1 John 5:1) and in what he did for us when he died (1 Corinthians 15:3-4). It also means believing by turning our back on sin (Acts 3:19) and sincerely making him our Leader (Galatians 2:20). Information and intellectual acceptance isn't enough. He wants us to trust him completely.

YOUR TURN

Jesus died so each of us could be rescued from spiritual death. He serves as a bridge between us and life. Do you believe in Jesus Christ? Belief is not simply acknowledging that Jesus once lived; it is affirming Jesus as the One you rely on above all. This is the most important decision you'll ever make! It sets the tone for all others that follow, for once you believe in Jesus, you begin a special relationship with him. Bobby Richardson, a former professional baseball player, explained it this way:

In my ten years of playing baseball for the New York Yankees I've received numerous letters from people all over the United States.... Many of these commend me for work with young people, and on being a fine religious person. Some even go on to make some statement such as, "I wish I could be like you but I guess I'm just made differently. I've tried religion and it doesn't work for me."

No, religion doesn't work, and it never will. There are many different religions which people have tried. Some of these are even called "Christian" religions. If I were to lead people to think "religion" or a good life bring peace and eternal life, it would be hypocrisy. All I can truly offer to others is a living Savior, Jesus Christ. Knowing him is a reality and it is he alone who offers salvation, not any religious system.

True Christianity is not escapism, nor a means to gain one's way to heaven by good works, but involvement with a living Person, Jesus Christ. God's Word says, "For it is by grace you have been saved, through faith—and this not from yourselves, it is the gift of God—not by works, so that no one can boast" (Ephesians 2:8-9).[1]

Bobby Richardson is saying that just being good or following religious rules isn't enough. We need to believe in Jesus Christ to save us, change us, and lead us every day. As a child, I knew some things about God. I went to church with my family. I prayed, and thought I was a pretty good kid. But something was missing. God seemed very far away, in spite of my efforts. When I was fourteen, I went to a Youth for Christ meeting in Kansas City, Kansas. For the first time, I realized what was missing: I needed to receive

Jesus' security and leadership in my life. That night I made my first decision to believe in him—the first of thousands to follow!

JESUS GIVES US A SECURE L I F E

When you go to a party and meet someone new, it's natural to ask, "Who are you?" or "What do you do?" Most people will respond by giving their occupation (student, businessman, homemaker) or a primary relationship (Jim's girlfriend, Sarah's brother, Tom's roommate). These answers are too often superficial. I have a friend who boldly replies, "I'm a child of God!" He gets some funny looks, but he is proclaiming the truth!

If you believe in Jesus, you're a transformed person, invigorated with the power of God. This has everything to do with the confidence needed to make quality decisions. You have a secure inner life—one that isn't ultimately dependent on your friends, family, or even your own efforts. L I F E is a useful mnemonic for understanding our most important identity, for remembering what Jesus gives us. Believers in Jesus are filled with LIFE:

Love… Each person has a deep, built-in need for belonging, for love. We need to feel we are part of someone else—that we are acceptable, respectable, even desirable to others. Our parents and friends often try to fill this need, never succeeding perfectly. Instead, most love is conditional upon our performance, meaning we will be loved if we measure up, appear attractive, or perform well.

But the love of Jesus is very different. Jesus loves us just as we are and not as we should be. It's a love we can't earn. Titus 3:4-6 emphasizes this fact: "But when the kindness and love of God our

Savior appeared, he saved us, not because of righteous things we had done, but because of his mercy. He saved us through the washing of rebirth and renewal by the Holy Spirit, whom he poured out on us generously through Jesus Christ our Savior." And in the assurance of God's love within us we can find energy, hope, and enthusiasm like we've never known before!

Inspiration... When we believe in Jesus, we receive more than just a hope and a new identity. We also receive the Holy Spirit (1 Corinthians 3:16-17; Ephesians 1:13-14). Part of God himself comes to live within us, giving us the gifts and energy we need to lead exceptional lives, as 2 Timothy 1:7 reminds us: "For God did not give us a spirit of timidity, but a spirit of power, of love and of self-discipline." It's not just a feeling, but a reality—the reality of God working within us. And this is inspiration in its most potent sense!

The Holy Spirit gives us the strength and ability to overcome life's obstacles. Inspiration refers to our sense of competence or, rather, our confidence in our potential to succeed. A sense of competence is another basic human need. People with a strong sense of competence are better able to handle life's many demands. A lack of this sense is at the heart of many psychological and social problems.

Forgiveness... Sin against God, others, and even ourselves is a sad fact of life. Most of us experience this reality through feelings of guilt and shame. We try hard to overcome these feelings through pleasurable diversions, self-sacrifice, or by performing well in our work and activities. But sin is still a burden we carry throughout our lives. Jesus wants to lift this burden from us; it can't be done through our own efforts. No amount of performance, escapism, or giving can pay off our spiritual debt.

But when we trust Jesus to do this, remarkable things happen. Spiritually, we become daughters and sons of God—and we're free from all liability to him. Mentally, we have the strongest reasons possible to experience relief from the guilt and shame associated with sin. Socially, we receive the foundation for intimate relationships with other believers, and all the potential benefits that go with these relationships.

Colossians 2:13-14 vividly describes the forgiveness we receive through Jesus: "When you were dead in your sins and in the uncircumcision of your sinful nature, God made you alive with Christ. He forgave us all our sins, having canceled the written code, with its regulations, that was against us and that stood opposed to us; he took it away, nailing it to the cross." Our account with God has been totally and permanently cleared by Jesus! We don't need to carry a burden of guilt any longer.

Eternity… In our teens and twenties, life seems so long, with so much potential for growth and rich experiences. But in the thirties and beyond, a sobering reality usually sets in—the reality that life will not last forever. Friends and parents begin to die, many education and career dreams become unfulfillable, and our hair becomes gray and skin wrinkled. For people who have no anticipation of life after death, depression and a sense of pointlessness become common, and even understandable.

But for those of us who believe in Jesus, the reality is much different. In 1 Peter 1:3-4, we read, "Praise be to the God and Father of our Lord Jesus Christ! In his great mercy he has given us new birth into a living hope through the resurrection of Jesus

Christ from the dead, and into an inheritance that can never perish, spoil or fade—kept in heaven for you." We have every reason for hope and anticipation in this life and beyond! Our dreams for family or career may never become reality in this life but God promises us a wonderful life forever and ever in heaven with him, and with one another. Grasping hold of this truth can give us remarkable courage, perspective, and enthusiasm in the midst of this life's setbacks.

Our secure position in Jesus is not just a warm, abstract feeling: It's a fact! Ours is a performance-oriented world. In fact, this is a performance-oriented book. But at the heart, performance is not most important—our identity is. *Doing* is not the standard of success—*who we are on the inside* is what makes life truly worthwhile.

This is a great paradox. The most essential thing in life—the security of Jesus—is not something we can achieve by striving in our own effort. Rather, it's a gift we can freely receive—we need only reach out and accept it.

Our identity in Jesus is the only adequate basis for our performance. Most people's motivation for performing is to give them a sense of self-esteem and self-worth. They are making a deliberate effort to "become somebody." In contrast, we already *are* somebody! As Christians, our motivation for work isn't to overcome a sense of inadequacy, guilt, or desperation. Rather, we work because we are grateful to Jesus and because he has given us LIFE, and this results in a strong sense of self-esteem and self-worth. Our performance becomes an expression of our security—a loving response to Jesus who will never leave us (Matthew 28:20), regardless of our success or failure. If there is any reason to sense direction, freedom, and enthusiasm for life, this is it!

NEW ON CAMPUS

Let me give you a personal account of how being secure in my identity in Jesus affected my decision-making in college. My first semester at the University of Missouri–Kansas City was one of the most difficult times of my life. I'd gone from being a popular class leader and extracurricular wonder at Park Hill High School, about twenty miles away, to the huge, impersonal university campus where I was known by little more than my social security number. I felt lonely for friends, intimidated by the difficult classes, and I endured a huge sense of loss in the transition from high school to university.

Just before winter vacation, a couple of friends invited me to a New Year's Eve party. *This is my big break,* I thought. *I'll get to meet a lot of people and break out of this rut.* I began counting the days.

When the big night arrived, I was ready: I wore a new shirt and had taken a good nap before leaving. I wasn't disappointed. The house was packed. The music was loud and everybody was talking. I felt great and jumped into a conversation.

"Hey, Nicholas," a friend called out to me. "Have you met Jill?"

"Jill?" I replied. "No, who's she?"

"She's the one putting on this party. This is her house. And you know what else? She's a knockout!"

Just then a girl walked up to us. It was Jill. My friend introduced us.

"Hi, Nicholas," she said. She had a soft, warm voice. "I'm glad you're here. I hope you have a good time!" She pinched my arm and walked away.

"You know what?" my friend exclaimed, "I think she likes you! I'd give anything to go out with her."

The rest of the evening I noticed Jill looking at me occasionally. *It would be great to get to know her*, I thought. Midnight came and everyone kissed his or her date. I felt a soft hand behind me and turned to find her embrace. She gave me a long, sweet kiss. We began to slow dance.

"I really like you," Jill whispered. I was trembling. "Ever since I first saw you at school I've liked you." She held me tighter. "When the others leave, I want you to stay. I want to go to bed with you!"

I felt weak in the knees but managed to keep dancing. "Jill, I like you, too. I'd really like to get to know you..." I paused a moment. "But I don't want to sleep with you."

Jill pulled back, surprised. "You don't? Then you must think I'm ugly!"

"No, no. It's not that. You're beautiful. I don't want to because I believe in Jesus. I'm going to wait until I'm married."

Jill was quiet and looked confused. We continued to dance. Finally she said, "Nobody has ever said that to me. All the guys just want to get me into bed." She was quiet again.

I thought for a moment, then asked, "Some of us are going canoeing Saturday afternoon. Why don't you come with us?" Her voice was sweet again. "I'd like that!"

OUR LEADER: JESUS CHRIST

Choosing to believe in Jesus isn't just a decision. Rather, it's a multitude of decisions to continue believing in him and obeying him day after day—decisions like my choice to wait for sex until marriage. If we cling to Jesus as our Security, we will also look to him as our Leader. Sure we continue to be influenced by friends, professors, and people at work. But Jesus Christ is our Commander, day after day, year after year.

Jesus is concerned about our decisions. Ephesians 5:15-16 reminds us to, "Be very careful, then, how you live—not as unwise but as wise, making the most of every opportunity, because the days are evil." Jesus refers to those who make foolish choices when he said, "But everyone who hears these words of mine and does not put them into practice is like a foolish man who built his house on sand. The rain came down, the streams rose, and the winds blew and beat against that house, and it fell with a great crash" (Matthew 7:26-27).

Paul, a powerful religious boss, at one time opposed Jesus and his followers at every opportunity. But after he understood who Jesus really is, and made him the Leader of his life, Paul's life direction changed completely. Part of his mission was to spread the gospel (Romans 1:15; 1 Corinthians 9:16). Everywhere he went, no matter who stood in his way, Paul told others about Jesus and his message. Another part of Paul's mission was to establish churches among the new believers (Acts 19:8-10). He spent years traveling and doing exactly that. Afterward, he continued to visit these churches and to encourage the development of their faith. Paul also worked to promote harmony among believers by giving advice, settling disputes, and distributing gifts to help those in need (Acts 15:2-22, 11:27-30).

Jesus talks about people like Paul in Matthew 7:24-25: "Therefore everyone who hears these words of mine and puts them into practice is like a wise man who built his house on the rock. The rain came down, the streams rose, and the winds blew and beat against that house; yet it did not fall, because it had its foundation on the rock."

Let's look at another man who made Jesus Christ his Leader. William Borden, heir to the fortune of the Borden family, had everything. He lived in New England in the late nineteenth century. Borden became an earnest Christian and was a brilliant student. He attended Yale University and was expected to join his brothers in the business empire the family had built.

However, Borden had a different allegiance. Instead of going on to business school, he attended Princeton Seminary. He was determined to help Muslims believe in Jesus Christ. Much to the regret of family and friends, he sailed to Cairo, Egypt, at age twenty-five. Borden spoke with vigor about Jesus to the people of that city. But tragically, he died a short time later of meningitis.

Did Borden waste his life? Not at all, for though he died young, he used his precious years for the most important business on earth—to make Jesus known. Borden, like his friends, was influenced by a variety of people. But he *believed* in Jesus Christ. For him, it was more than a single decision; it was a lifestyle. He changed completely! Borden's belief influenced his decision to leave his wealth, family, and friends, so that others could know the same truth!

One-time decisions often are cheap, and the cost of truly believing may seem high. But like William Borden, you and I need to follow Jesus every day, in every situation. When we do this, our individual decisions get off to a great start!

TAKE ACTION!

1)   List the people, by name, who influence you the most. This might include your parents, teachers, friends, or characters on a favorite TV program.

2)   How does Jesus fit into your life? Do you need to rethink your relationship with him?

3)   Ask some people that you know believe in Jesus Christ why they made that decision.

4)   Can you identify a major decision you've made that was influenced by your faith in Jesus?

CHAPTER FOUR

How Does God Lead Us?

O nce we believe in Jesus and intentionally make him the leader of our lives, we naturally want to know what he says we should do. But how does God guide us? Many people feel confused or uncertain in their understanding of this important matter. Let me give you some examples.

• Tim was in his sophomore year on a football scholarship. He really enjoyed playing football. The deadline for declaring his degree major was coming up but Tim wasn't sure whether to major in physical education, like many of his teammates, or in business. He felt a business degree would help him find a job more easily, but he really wasn't sure which major he should choose.

Finally, he devised a plan. The Super Bowl was coming up the following week. Tim thought this would be a good opportunity for God to show him what to do. So he prayed, "God, if you want me to major in PE, have the Dallas Cowboys win. If they lose, I'll know it's your will for me to study business." When the Cowboys came up short, Tim signed up for business. He was confident it was God's leading.

Tim began the next semester with excitement. But the classes seemed boring and lengthy, and he didn't seem to fit in with the rest of the students. Worst of all, Tim's grades were barely passing. By the end of the semester, he decided he couldn't trust the Cowboys *or* God. Tim switched back to physical education studies.

• Margaret was about to finish graduate school. For years she had planned to become a missionary. But she didn't know in which country she should work. One day she was walking down a road and praying about this decision. Suddenly, she noticed a pretty rock and picked it up. It was shaped like Africa. Margaret exclaimed out loud, "God is saying I should go to Africa!"

She applied to a mission organization, was accepted, and flew to Africa. The first term was very hard for her. Margaret found it difficult to understand the language and customs of the nationals, and mail and financial support from America were scarce. She began to have second thoughts about her decision. "If I had held up the rock another way, it would have looked like England," Margaret speculated aloud. "Perhaps God really meant to send me to England!"

• David and Carol met at a party. He was really excited about her, and asked her out for the following Saturday. They flew kites together and then went for pizza. David couldn't seem to keep his eyes off Carol, and several times told her how pretty she was. As they were eating, David announced, "Carol, it's God's will for us to be married."

Carol nearly choked on her crust! "Why do you say that?" she asked in alarm.

"I prayed about it all week," David said. "God has given me a strong peaceful feeling that you're the one! That's his sign to me!"

Carol gasped, "If you're so sure God is leading us, why hasn't he given me the same feeling? Besides, we just met last week!"

After that night, Carol felt very uncomfortable around David. She never went out with him again.

SHOW US THE WAY!

We trust God and want his help to make our decisions. In fact, there may be danger in not receiving his guidance. Proverbs 14:12 reminds us, "There is a way that seems right to a man, but in the end it leads to death." Christians often talk about the will of God. How we understand God's guidance can greatly influence our attitude (fatalistic, submissive, relaxed, responsible), our decision-making (passive, active), and our actions (apathetic, hard working).

God wants us to know his will. Ephesians 5:17 tells us, "Therefore do not be foolish, but understand what the Lord's will is." His will is not meant to be a secret! Paul wrote to his friends, "...we have not stopped praying for you and asking God to fill you with the knowledge of his will through all spiritual wisdom and understanding. And we pray this in order that you may live a life worthy of the Lord and may please him in every way: bearing fruit in every good work, growing in the knowledge of God" (Colossians 1:9-10).

God *will* guide us. But Tim, Margaret, Carol, and many more of us feel uncertain just how this happens. Let's look at two important ways.

GOD'S GENERAL GUIDANCE—FOR EVERYONE!

God gives us *general guidance*—"general" in that it is for each and every person. The terms "moral" or "desired" will of God have similar meanings. We can understand the general will of God primarily through the teachings of the Bible. In 2 Timothy 3:16-17 we read, "All Scripture is God-breathed and is useful for teaching, rebuking, correcting and training in righteousness, so that the man of God may be thoroughly equipped for every good work." God has already shared with us his general will. It includes the following:

- God desires that all people be saved (1 Timothy 2:3-4; 2 Peter 3:9).
- He wants us to thank him (1 Thessalonians 5:18).
- God desires that we show mercy to one another and resolve conflicts (Matthew 5:7-9).
- He urges us to be careful with our speech (James 3:9-10).
- He wants us to give cheerfully (2 Corinthians 9:7).
- God wants us to care for those who are less fortunate than we are (James 1:27).
- He desires for us to pray for one another's spiritual growth (Colossians 1:9-10).
- God expects us to remain morally pure (1 Thessalonians 4:1-3).
- He wants believers to meet together and to encourage one another (Hebrews 10:25).

You see, God already has provided for us many biblical principles and specific instructions. This helps to answer many of our questions. But as Psalm 119:97 reminds us, we must read the Bible to know God's general will!

SOMETIMES GOD GUIDES US INDIVIDUALLY

The Bible doesn't address details of every situation, such as specifically whom to marry, where to go to school, or with whom to be friends. It doesn't tell us whether to buy a stereo or a camera with our spare cash. Neither does it reveal where to go on vacation or what to wear when we get there. Will God help us with individual decisions?

There are some instances recorded in the Bible in which God gave individuals instructions through an audible voice, a trance or vision, a dream, prophecy, miracle, or by means of an angelic messenger (Matthew 1:20, 2:12-13, 2:19-20; Acts 10:3-8, 10:9-20, 16:9-10, 18:9-11, 22:17-21, 23:11, 27:23-25). For example, in Acts 9:1-19, Jesus appeared to Paul in a vision and told him to go into Damascus. At about the same time, Jesus also appeared to a disciple named Ananias and told him exactly where to find Paul. Clearly, this was a spectacular event!

Sometimes God guides individual Christians in special ways. What is remarkable about these biblical accounts, however, is that they were supernatural. God's guidance didn't depend on things such as emotions, circumstances, or impressions. When God directed, he did it in such a way that there was no doubt about his meaning.

THE POPULAR VIEW OF GUIDANCE

Apart from the Bible's general guidance and supernaturally delivered instructions, does God guide individuals in any other ways? This is a critical question. The most popular view among evangelical Christians is that, yes, God will tell us exactly what to do anytime we ask him to. To discover his individual guidance we must read "road signs" that God gives us to point the way.

These are not usually miraculous signs. Instead, the individual will of God is thought to be revealed through means such as a feeling of inner peace (Philippians 4:6-7; Colossians 3:15); an inward voice or impression (1 Kings 19:12; Isaiah 30:21; John 10:27); and circumstances that indicate direction (Isaiah 7:10-14, 37:30-32; Matthew 16:1-4). This popular view also emphasizes that guidance must be consistent with Bible teaching and mature counsel.

Some believe God's guidance is so complete that he has a perfect, detailed plan for each person's life. Ideally, God has already chosen the person we will marry, what car model we should buy, and what we will eat for breakfast. If we miss finding his individual guidance, then we are left with second best—sometimes called the "permissive" will of God. To discover his perfect plan, according to this view, we must continuously and correctly read the "road signs" showing which way to go.

The popular conception of God's leading is illustrated in the life of Andrew, a high school junior. Andrew had begun making plans for college. Fortunately, he had just attended a church workshop on decision-making and the will of God. Andrew was convinced God had already selected a college for him. So he began to look for God's signs to point him the right way.

Andrew's father was a professor at the local university, Billboard State. And as his son, Andrew could attend for one-half the normal tuition. Besides, other schools were far away. Andrew viewed this circumstance as a sign from God that he should attend his father's school. When Andrew talked with his friends and youth pastor, they all encouraged him to attend Billboard.

He also had a growing impression and peace that he should stay home for college. These last two signs were the final confirmation Andrew was expecting. He was convinced God was showing him specifically where to go to school, so he enrolled at Billboard State with confidence.

ON THE OTHER HAND...

The story of Andrew and Billboard University sounds familiar, even comforting, to many of us. But does God really act in this way? There are several problems with the popular view. I'd like to explore some of them with you.

The biblical support is questionable. Verses frequently cited for individual guidance include: Psalm 32:8; Isaiah 30:20-21; Romans 12:1-2; Ephesians 5:15-17; Colossians 1:9, 4:12. I believe these verses, in their proper context, do not point to individual guidance. Rather, they more precisely refer to God's general guidance, as expressed throughout the Bible.

While not necessarily true of the Scriptures listed above, I want to share with you how one Scripture has been misinterpreted. Proverbs 3:5-6 is one of the most frequently quoted references for individual guidance. The King James Version rendition of this passage reads, "Trust in the Lord with all thine heart, and lean not on thine own understanding. In all thy ways acknowledge him, and he shall direct thy paths."

Critical to understanding this verse is the phrase "...and he shall direct thy paths." Hebrew lexicons and scholarly studies more accurately reveal the meaning of the phrase in question to be: "...and God will make our paths smooth, straight, or successful." The New International Version better translates these words as "...and he will make your paths straight." The essence of Proverbs 3:5-6 is not that we will receive individual directions from God but that we who trust God's counsel will experience *success* (as defined by God's standard). Dr. Bruce Waltke reflects on his experience with this conclusion:

> All of us have had the shocking discovery that a favorite verse in the King James Version was inaccurate, and hence that we had been led into an inauthentic experience. I recall the astonishment of one of the committee members assigned to translate the Book of Proverbs for the New International Version when he discovered that Proverbs 3:5 had nothing to say about guidance. He had taken as his life text: "In all your ways acknowledge him and he will direct your paths." But when confronted with the linguistic data he had to admit reluctantly that the verse more properly read "...and he will make your path smooth."[1]

The problem of subjectivity. The written Word of God and supernatural revelation are straightforward. But the popular view of God's guidance is based largely upon subjective elements. Inner impressions, for example, are thought sometimes to be leadings from God. But they can also be influenced by Satan, emotional swings, medications, hormonal cycles, sleep deprivation, illness, and so on. We can never know for sure where our impressions are coming from!

Likewise, circumstances are hard to interpret. Is an opportunity, or "open door," a sign to act or is it rather a test of faith? Who provided the opportunity? God, Satan, someone else, or natural events? Is an obstacle another test of our commitment, or an indication to look elsewhere? The Bible tells us very little about how to interpret circumstances, beyond the insight gained by applying biblical principles to each situation.

The popular view also relies heavily upon reading our emotions, such as feelings of peace or anxiety, as indications from God. True, a mature Christian acting in violation of the truth will often experience guilt. But while a peaceful feeling may mean we're acting in concert with biblical teaching, this isn't always the case. Christians have peacefully gone into sin, and felt anxiety when doing the greatest good. Emotions are not reliable road maps. All of us have impressions, observe circumstances, and experience peace or anxiety. But while these factors may be considered in decision-making, the Bible doesn't promise they are individual signs from God.

There are some practical problems with the popular view. One of these is the matter of daily decisions. Most of us must make so many decisions every day (what to wear, when to leave, whom to talk with, how to spend our money) that it seems impossible to seek out God's individual guidance in every small choice. Realistically, the popular view can only be applied to major decisions.

Another problem is that this view may foster immaturity. Too many believers find comfort in the idea that God has already made their decisions for them, so they never develop good judgment or planning skills. Foolish decisions are justified with, "But I know God called me to do this." People who take such positions are seldom open to input from others, holding that "no one can argue with God." Unfortunately, individual divine guidance is used to support many tragic choices.

Besides, how many different "road signs" must agree before a person can be sure of individual guidance? Must they all agree? Is five out of six enough? Isn't God able to make himself clear through one means of communication? And what should be done when two believers claim to receive conflicting guidance over a joint decision? Is one of them not reading God correctly? Is God giving them conflicting messages? The Bible doesn't address these subjects directly.

Christians who hold the popular view are usually very sincere and earnest in their faith. But many of them are frustrated, filled with doubt over correctly interpreting God's leading. Guilt often follows when they must act without assurance. They also waste valuable time and energy seeking individual guidance, when this position cannot be biblically confirmed.

Few Christians are willing to express criticism with the popular view, lest they be labeled as divisive. But we must reexamine this teaching that is so deeply rooted in our churches. A detailed critique of the popular view is beyond the scope of this book. Instead, I refer you to the eloquent presentation by Gary Friesen, of Multnomah School of the Bible, and J. Robin Maxson, in their book, *Decision Making and the Will of God: A Biblical Alternative to the Traditional View*.[2]

HOW SHOULD WE THEN DECIDE?

God may supernaturally communicate with us and if he does, we should certainly obey. But supernatural revelations seem to be rare events. So we are back at where we began: How shall we make decisions? Let's look at what was done in the days of the early churches.

First, we find a problem in the church at Jerusalem (Acts 6:1-6). Not everyone was receiving his or her share of food. The apostles asked the believers to choose seven men to resolve the conflict. "This proposal pleased the whole group," we are told, so this group chose the men who seemed best—with no mention of any individual guidance from God.

Later, in the church at Antioch, the believers were worshipping the Lord and fasting. The Holy Spirit said to them, "Set apart for me Barnabas and Saul [Paul] for the work to which I have called them" (Acts 13:2). So the two men went out to share the gospel, obeying this supernatural instruction. Little doubt lingered that this is what God wanted them to do. But we don't read that God gave Paul and Barnabas any other individual directions during their first journey.

After their trip, the two returned to the church at Antioch. Later, Paul said to Barnabas, "Let us go back and visit the brothers in all the towns where we preached the word of the Lord and see how they are doing" (Acts 15:36). As opposed to the first journey, no mention is made of any individual guidance from God. Neither is it recorded that God told Paul to make the third trip (Acts 18:23). Many other examples can be found of Christians making decisions with no mention of God showing them individually what to do: Acts 11:27-30, 15:34-40, 17:16-17, 20:16; Romans

1:10-13; 1 Corinthians 6:1-6, 7:37, 16:3-9; 2 Corinthians 1:15–2:4; Philippians 2:25-26; 1 Thessalonians 3:1-2. We cannot infer from this that God definitely did not provide individual guidance to these people, but Scripture does not record that He did.

These examples are instructive for us today. It appears that the first believers made almost all decisions based on the general will of God. There was rarely a special message, and no evidence they were expecting to receive the ones that came. Nor were they trying to discern God's individual leading by reading *today's* popular "road signs."

The first believers were simply following the general will of God, as it had been taught to them by Christ and the apostles. Occasionally God gave them some supernatural and individual directions (Acts records fifteen to twenty cases of direct individual guidance). However, I believe this to be the exception, not the norm. Most of the time, these people just made the best choices they were capable of making; they made them prayerfully and carefully, but on their own.

Like the early Christians, we too need to make our decisions as best we can, without expecting a sign from God. Pray and listen for the voice of God (for an excellent treatment of this topic, refer to Richard J. Foster's *Prayer: Finding the Heart's True Home—* Harper, 1992), then, following the guidelines presented in this book, take the plunge! Whom we marry, where we go to college, and what car we buy are *our* choices! God has given us tremendous freedom to select for ourselves, within the guidelines of his general will.

Friesen and Maxson write:

The question to which we are seeking a biblical answer is: In nonmoral (ethically neutral) areas, on what basis is the believer to make his decision? Observation of apostolic decision-making has revealed that they did not attempt to discover God's individual will for such decisions. Their explanations for their plans are couched in phrases such as: "We thought it best," "I thought it necessary," "If it is fitting," "It is not desirable," "It seemed good," and simply "I have decided" (Titus 3:12). (Luke explained a decision Paul made with respect to an itinerary with the words, "for he was hurrying" [Acts 20:16].) Clearly these men were exercising their freedom of choice within God's moral (general) will. But on what basis?

Perhaps the principle could be stated this way: In nonmoral decisions, the goal of the believer is to make decisions on the basis of spiritual expediency. In this statement, some definitions are important. "Spiritual" means that the ends in view, as well as the means to those ends, are governed by the moral will of God. In nonmoral decisions, as in every other aspect of life, the Christian's aim is to glorify and please God. In that sense, every goal and procedure is to be "spiritual." "Expediency" refers to the quality of being suitable or advantageous to the end in view. Put simply, it means what works best to get the job done—within God's moral will, of course.[3]

The realization of freedom is a relief to many believers, as it was to me. For years I tried to follow the popular view, rarely certain of the definite leadings my friends claimed they experienced. At first I thought this was because I was not spiritual enough. But then I discovered that even Christian leaders had similar questions. A better understanding of God's leading steered me to a fresh approach to living—not on the basis of some obscure heavenly plan but by the wise application of biblical principles. This was particularly important as I wrestled with deciding if I should work in Angola. Did God tell me individually what to do? I don't think so. But it was clear that both sharing about Jesus and caring for the sick are part of God's general will for all Christians. A decision to go would certainly be consistent with my faith.

Free choice has always been part of God's plan, along with voluntary faith and obedience to God. In Genesis 2:16-17 we read that God told the original couple, Adam and Eve, to eat fruit from any tree but one. Hundreds of trees must have bloomed fragrantly. What a choice! In the early church a question was debated over whether to eat meat that had been sacrificed to idols (Romans 14:13-23; 1 Corinthians 8, 10:23-33). Paul told these Christians they should decide for *themselves* what to do. The only principles to be mindful of were to love one another and not cause others to stumble. Paul made it clear that many decisions are simply up to us to make, and that we are responsible for our choices (Romans 14:1-6, 10, 12).

Does this freedom mean God can't be bothered with our small affairs? Does it indicate he doesn't care about our decisions? No, that isn't true at all. He loves us, comforts us, gives us strength and eternal life. He cares about each decision, no matter how seemingly insignificant. This is why he has given us general direction. But God gives us the privilege and responsibility to choose for ourselves in most situations. God has called us to peace, to love, to share the Good News, and to live righteously. It's up to us to work out the details.

TAKE ACTION!

1)   How have you looked at God's leading in the past?

2)   Has your view of God's guidance been challenged or confirmed by what you have just read? In what ways?

3)   Do you need to change your thinking about God's guidance? If so, how?

PART TWO

OUR
MISSION:

To Love Jesus, Others, & Yourself

CHAPTER FIVE

The Five P's

Matt was a psychology major at a northwestern university. The spring of his junior year had been busy. He was exhausted by midsemester exams, and was thinking about the break coming up soon—a week of freedom! Matt was excited about the prospect of getting out of the class routine for a few days. But he wasn't sure what to do during vacation.

His friends also were looking forward to the break. Matt's roommate was a pharmacy major. He had worked out a job with a local pharmacy. During the break, he figured he could earn enough to buy a stereo. Matt usually had lunch with another psych major who was running for class president the coming year. This friend wanted the position badly, and asked Matt to help him make campaign posters during break. But this didn't interest Matt very much.

Another option Matt had was to paint his car. This was a project he had been putting off too long. On top of these possibilities, some of Matt's friends invited him to go to the beach for the week. This sounded like the best plan yet!

Two weeks before his last exam, the pastor at Matt's church talked about relationships. He said loving others was the Christian's highest objective. The pastor also challenged the congregation to look for practical ways to do this. Afterward, Matt spoke with one of his friends, Kristen.

"What sort of plans do you have for vacation?" she asked.

"Well, I'm not really sure. Maybe I'll go to the beach with some buddies."

"That sounds like fun," said Kristen. "I've found something I really enjoy, too. I work at a crisis center in my spare time."

"What's that?" asked Matt with interest.

"It's where people can call on the telephone when they have trouble. Some are kids who are high on drugs. Others are people wanting to kill themselves. Elderly people call, too, just to talk."

"That sounds interesting. But isn't it a lot of responsibility?" asked Matt.

"Sometimes it is. But I get real satisfaction from knowing I'm helping. With spring break, most of our volunteers are leaving for vacation... I wonder, would you be interested in helping during those days? There's a counselor training course starting Tuesday."

Matt paused a moment. He looked thoughtfully at his pastor, who was talking with a small group of people across the room. "Yes. I'll do it."

A few weeks later, Matt was talking with his friends who had gone to the beach. They were tanned and tired. When they asked why he hadn't gone, Matt told them the truth. Some laughed. They said he'd wasted his time.

Matt just smiled and said, "There was a thirteen-year-old kid who'd run away from home. He was scared and lost. He called me at the crisis center and told me he wanted to go home, but he didn't have a way to get back to Chicago. We lined up a bus ticket for him. And a man called who was holding a gun to his head. He wanted help, so we talked about his problems. He put down his gun and went to the hospital."

His friends weren't impressed, but Matt didn't waver from believing he'd made the right choice. "Look, guys...I don't have a sunburn, but I've never had such an awesome time in my life!"

MISSION TO PLANET EARTH

Before we decide what to do today, it's important to decide what to do this month. But before we decide about the month, we need to think about the year. And before we decide what to do this year, we really need to ask, "What is my mission in life?" Our mission, or purpose, is our foremost objective. It's the "big picture" of what we are doing. When people say they want to be successful in business or to be rich and famous, they are describing purpose. Similarly, when we talk about winning the world for Christ or living like Jesus, we're making statements of purpose.

It's important to understand our mission in life. An ancient Oriental proverb states, "He who aims at nothing, hits it." This is still true! Our mission gives direction for our decisions and efforts. It becomes the basis for creating specific action plans. Mission helps prevent us from becoming distracted and wasting time. It inspires us when we feel uncertain about what to do or when we are dissatisfied with the seeming humdrum of life. Mission keeps us thinking about future possibilities and helps take the emphasis off our past. It gives us a sense of identity and confidence in who we are and what we're doing in life. Mission also helps us socially, giving us words to express our beliefs to others, and a sense of oneness with those who share our vision.

Most of us have difficulty thinking about this subject. We're not used to dealing with such big ideas. It's easier to discuss our lives in terms of our profession or career. But is this adequate? No, I don't think so. To sum up our reason for existing and working in such shallow terms is to cheat ourselves. There's far more to life than work!

The apostle Paul knew his mission. He said, "Forgetting what is behind and straining toward what is ahead, I press on toward the goal to win the prize for which God has called me heavenward in Christ Jesus" (Philippians 3:13-14). His mission gave direction for his life. What is your mission?

John Boykin, senior editor for *Stanford* magazine, emphasized the modern significance of purpose when he wrote, "By knowing the purpose our Creator has for us, we can make better sense of his Word, his will, and his workings in our lives, and can more intelligently respond by setting our priorities according to that purpose. Knowing our purpose is also the only basis for assessing whether or not we are working right."[1]

When you read a book, you look for the theme. What is the book about? In the same way, when we each examine our own life, we need to look for our *life* theme. What are we aiming for? There are several purposes to choose from. Let's look at them. They are what I call the *five P's*.

POSSESSIONS

One purpose you can choose for your life is to acquire money and possessions. This is a popular notion in western countries like America, but it's present everywhere. I was talking to a group of teenagers one day in a rural African village. They lived in mud-block houses, wore rags, and were very fortunate if they even owned a bicycle. I asked, "What's the biggest problem among people your age?" I was shocked when one replied, "Materialism. People here live only for what they can get—like a new shirt or a radio."

Of course, we all need certain possessions—such as clothes, cars, and houses. The concept of personal property is supported biblically and legally. Still, there is strong pressure to make possessions the most important aspect of existence. Many people don't feel they amount to much until they have a nice house, a new stereo, beautiful clothes, two cars in the garage, and a boat on the lake.

Is there more to life than amassing possessions? In Luke 12:16-21 we find Jesus telling a story to those who thought money was the most important thing in life:

"The ground of a certain rich man produced a good crop. He thought to himself, 'What shall I do? I have no place to store my crops.'

"Then he said, 'This is what I'll do. I will tear down my barns and build bigger ones, and there I will store all my grain and my goods. And I'll say to myself, "You have plenty of good things laid up for many years. Take life easy; eat, drink and be merry." '

"But God said to him, 'You fool! This very night your life will be demanded from you. Then who will get what you have prepared for yourself?'

"This is how it will be with anyone who stores up things for himself but is not rich toward God."

We all need possessions. But we're deluded when we begin to define our self-esteem and sense of personal success by what we have, for, "A man's life does not consist in the abundance of his possessions" (Luke 12:15). When possessions get in the way of more important things, there can be trouble!

POSITION

Many people seek position, finding authority and power attractive. For example, though most university professors are not paid well, those positions command much respect. Therefore they're appealing. Likewise, pastors and missionaries are not well paid in terms of cash, but are highly looked upon by most in the Christian community. Some students want to be class president, a member of the varsity basketball team, or valedictorian. After graduating from college, these same people may want to become an airline captain, president of a successful company, or chairman of a board. Is gaining a powerful position a worthwhile purpose?

King Herod had a high position with absolute authority over the people of Palestine. He answered only to the emperor of the Roman Empire. Maintaining his powerful position was essential to Herod. In Matthew, chapter 2, we read that some important people, the Magi, came from far away to worship baby Jesus. They went to Herod and asked, "Where is the one who has been born king of the Jews?"

Herod became very disturbed when he heard this question. *He* was king of the Jews! Who was the baby prophesied to replace him? Herod wanted to know where this baby could be found! When the Magi didn't help him, he took the situation into his own hands and killed all the boys in Bethlehem and its vicinity who were two years old and younger. Maintaining Herod's power was, to him, worth the lives of many children.

The apostle Paul also held a prominent position. He was an educated religious leader. Paul was respected by the people of his day and led the persecution against Christians. But he gave it all up after he found something far more important than power. Paul explained this in Philippians 3:7-8, "But whatever was to my profit I now consider loss for the sake of Christ. What is more, I consider everything a loss compared to the surpassing greatness of knowing Christ Jesus my Lord, for whose sake I have lost all things. I consider them rubbish, that I may gain Christ."

We must have good leaders in positions of power. Without this, our churches, governments, and businesses would surely fail. Yet position only for positions sake is an empty goal at the least, and often a precursor of evil. There's more to life than position, isn't there?

PLEASURE

Pleasure is another great driving force. People want to be comfortable and entertained. So we have clubs, beaches, alcohol, sports, art, music, and so forth. We want to experience the satisfying sensations that pleasure can bring. But should personal pleasure be our primary objective?

Parties and good times are an important part of life. When the prodigal son finally came home to his loving father, a grand festival was held, with music, dancing, fine clothes, and good food. His return was something wonderful to celebrate!

Yet pleasure for the wrong reason can have a dark side. In the book of Daniel, we read of a great feast given by King Belshazzar for a thousand nobles:

> So they brought in the gold goblets that had been taken from the temple of God in Jerusalem, and the king and his nobles, his wives and his concubines drank from them. As they drank the wine, they praised the gods of gold and silver, of bronze, iron, wood and stone.
>
> Suddenly the fingers of a human hand appeared and wrote on the plaster of the wall, near the lampstand in the royal palace. The king watched the hand as it wrote. His face turned pale and he was so frightened that his knees knocked together and his legs gave way (Daniel 5:3-6).

The prophet Daniel interpreted the message to the king, which pronounced God's judgment on him. Later that night the city was captured and the king killed. What a way to end a party!

We all need recreation and some comforts. Life would be very difficult without time for relaxation. But isn't there more to life than just pursuing personal pleasure?

PROJECTS

Some people center their lives around projects or tasks, such as building companies, designing bridges, constructing model cars, and writing books. Other projects are nonmaterial, like finishing college, running a five-minute mile, or helping elect a political candidate. Some people get a real sense of satisfaction from finishing a project. But is it worthwhile to build our lives around projects alone?

Many years after Solomon's original temple was destroyed, King Herod of Palestine had it rebuilt to please the people. It took forty-six years to complete and was one marvel of the ancient world—a magnificent structure! In Matthew 24:1-2 we read, "Jesus left the temple and was walking away when his disciples came up to him to call his attention to its buildings. 'Do you see all these things?' he asked. 'I tell you the truth, not one stone here will be left on another; every one will be thrown down.' "

This great project didn't impress Jesus a bit! His only concern was for a much different purpose. We, too, can give ourselves to many projects, and even accomplish them. But Jesus is not primarily interested in these. If a great temple built for the worship of God didn't impress him, what would?

HAVING IT ALL

Let's look at a man who had all it all: possessions, position, pleasure, and projects. It was King Solomon. Chapter 10 of 1 Kings describes him as the richest, wisest, and most powerful man of his time. Yet, what did he think of himself? Solomon wrote in Ecclesiastes 2:3-11:

> I wanted to see what was worthwhile for men to do under
> heaven during the few days of their lives. I undertook great
> projects: I built houses for myself and planted vineyards. I
> made gardens and parks and planted all kinds of fruit trees in
> them. I made reservoirs to water groves of flourishing trees. I

bought male and female slaves and had other slaves who were born in my house. I also owned more herds and flocks than anyone in Jerusalem before me. I amassed silver and gold for myself, and the treasure of kings and provinces. I acquired men and women singers, and a harem as well—the delights of the heart of man. I became greater by far than anyone in Jerusalem before me. In all this my wisdom stayed with me. I denied myself nothing my eyes desired; I refused my heart no pleasure. My heart took delight in all my work, and this was the reward for all my labor.

Yet when I surveyed all that my hands had done and what I had toiled to achieve, everything was meaningless, a chasing after the wind; nothing was gained under the sun.

Now look at his last statement. This is the message of the man who had it all: position, possessions, projects, and pleasure. He still wasn't satisfied.

Many of us aren't satisfied, either. We carefully plan our lives, work hard, gain some recognition, and still feel an emptiness deep inside, as if we're missing something; or we experience the hope-lessness that comes from concluding that there's nothing more to life. What *are* we missing?

PEOPLE

Jesus is our Leader. What does He say about our mission? Jesus was talking to a crowd of people, as recorded in Matthew 22:35-40, when someone asked a question that enabled the Lord to get to the heart of our purpose in life:

One of them, an expert in the law, tested him with this question: "Teacher, which is the greatest commandment in the Law?" Jesus replied: " 'Love the Lord your God with all your heart and with all your soul and with all your mind.' This is the first and greatest commandment. And the second is like it: 'Love your neighbor as yourself.' All the Law and the Prophets hang on these two commandments."

Jesus is saying that our mission is to love God, others, and as we'll see later, ourselves. This sums up all the teaching in the Bible. Nothing could be more simple.

Jesus' statement was challenging to the people of that time. They, like us, put their emphasis on the other four P's (possessions, position, projects, pleasure). But to Jesus Christ, how we relate to God, others, and ourselves is the best measure of our success in life. Matt discovered this truth at the crisis center.

People are the focus of Matthew 25:32-40, where Jesus is talking about the judgment of each person, and says:

All the nations will be gathered before him [Jesus Christ], and he will separate the people one from another as a shepherd separates the sheep from the goats. He will put the sheep on his right and the goats on his left.

Then the King will say to those on his right, "Come, you who are blessed by my Father; take your inheritance, the kingdom prepared for you since the creation of the world. For I was hungry and you gave me something to eat, I was thirsty and you gave me something to drink, I was a stranger and you invited me in, I needed clothes and you clothed me, I was sick and you looked after me, I was in prison and you came to visit me."

Then the righteous will answer him, "Lord, when did we see you hungry and feed you, or thirsty and give you something to drink? When did we see you a stranger and invite you in, or needing clothes and clothe you? When did we see you sick or in prison and go to visit you?"

The King will reply, "I tell you the truth, whatever you did for one of the least of these brothers of mine, you did for me."

Jesus goes on to talk about the goats as those people who didn't feed the hungry, give drink to the thirsty, or look after the sick. They are the ones who will be separated from God for eternity. You see, *the most important facet of life is how we treat people.* It's an expression of our faith. It's the barometer of our relationship with God.

Once I spoke before a class at Park Hill High School, where I had been a student. I asked each student in class to write on a piece of paper what he or she wanted to accomplish in life. Then I read their written responses aloud. All spoke about life's purpose in terms of career, with one exception. One boy wanted to have a good family life. This student was on the right track. True satisfaction comes from having a positive, lasting impact on the lives of people. If you live for any other purpose, you have sold yourself short.

THE NEW MAN AND WOMAN

Christians are not the only ones who have emphasized the importance of people. Karl Marx, writing in the midst of the

Industrial Revolution in Europe, saw the gross injustices forced on workers. He was so disturbed by what he witnessed that he began to form a philosophy which he postulated could elevate the common man. People, he reasoned, should work for the common good, not for possessions or power. They should be motivated just by knowing they are helping each other. What Marx envisioned was far more than an economic system; it was an entire philosophy and way of communal life.

Marx's ideas led to a political movement. He proposed a strong political party to uphold his philosophy and guide a central government. The goal of this government would be to control all production, employment, and commerce, eliminating unfair social classes and exploitation of workers. Marx visualized each person receiving a similar wage and benefiting equally from the steady social and economic progress of the country. What he said was very attractive to the oppressed people of his time and place.

Marx was intelligent. He knew there was no way such a society as he proposed could exist without a fundamental change in human nature. People needed to be liberated from their selfishness—to be transformed from egotistical, aggressive, greedy, and immoral people into new social beings. There needed to be strong laws to enforce equality until society became filled with such New Men and Women. New People, as he saw them, would be cooperative, loving, neighborly, and eager to share. Without this transformation, they could never attain true communism.

But how could such a fundamental change in human nature be brought about? Marx proposed transforming people by educating them in Marxist values. Once all were transformed, the people would hardly need a government. They would take care of themselves and each other automatically. He spoke very convincingly.

Has the Marxist philosophy and communist form of government succeeded? Has it fostered communities where people love one another and work for the common good? History answers this question with a resounding "No!" In recent years, the nations of Eastern Europe and Africa have thrown off Marxism. In China, where Marxism continues to reign as the official philosophy, the government is one of the most oppressive in history, causing untold human misery. In terms of human freedoms and economic progress, Marxist countries have failed.

Why is this? It's because of the difficulty of changing human nature. Numerous Marxist nations have been established, only to fail in their quest for social transformation and equality. Selfishness is hard to control, particularly for political leaders. They have tremendous power, and often use it to pursue personal possessions, position, pleasure, and projects. Lenin experienced this problem in Russia, in spite of nationwide Marxist education. He wrote, "The workers are building the new society without having turned themselves into New Men, who would be free from the dirt of the world. They are still up to their knees in it."[2]

While I lived in China, I witnessed the battle Marxists waged to control the minds of university students (see *Shanghai Doctor*, Zondervan, 1991). Their efforts were largely misguided and unsuccessful. The youth of China, as a whole, are just as possession- and position-oriented as any in the West, in spite of all the propaganda to the contrary.

People don't need a political or philosophical change as much as they need a spiritual change. And only Jesus Christ can make that happen. We who have faith in Jesus have the power to go beyond ourselves and love others because he loves us. This power was evident in the lives of the first Christians. They were transformed people! They ate their meals together and shared their possessions. They collected money to help those in need. They worshipped God together and were lights to their communities.

The Marxist denies God exists and doesn't have access to his life-changing power. Other efforts to change people are confounded by the same basic problem: selfishness. That's why God sent a Savior to us—Jesus Christ. He is the One who can rescue us from our selfishness. He is the One who can give us the right mission to live for, and the power to do it.

WHAT'S YOUR MISSION?

Let's look at our options again. We can work to gain an exalted position, to have possessions, to complete projects, to experience pleasure, and/or to build loving relationships with people. Actually, most people work toward achieving some combination of these. The purposes of many people look something like this:

- To be president of my company (position).
- To have a nice house and car (possessions).
- To have a happy relationship with my spouse (people).
- To finish building my wooden boat (projects).
- To vacation in Florida each year (pleasure).

Is there anything wrong with this list of purposes? Not necessarily. The problem is that the priority given to people is usually too low. People, while most important, often must compete with many other interests. We're so possession-oriented, position-conscious, and pleasure-pursuing that we let our relationships slip.

Am I saying there is no place for the other four P's? Absolutely not! We depend upon skilled leaders in high positions. We need certain possessions to help ease life's burdens. There are many worthy projects. We all need to relax and have fun. But people should *always* be our highest priority.

It is possible, when employing wisdom, to love people by *using* your position, possessions, projects, and even your pleasures. I'm interested in aviation and earned a pilot's license. I've used this skill to travel to work at distant hospitals and clinics, but most of my trips are to visit friends or family. One day I realized I was seldom using my aviation training for anyone else, so I began to pray for an opportunity to do so. A short time later, I learned that a fellow in my church named Steve was very ill with cancer. Like me, he was an avid pilot. But he was grounded by his illness. I called Steve to ask if he'd like to come flying, with me acting as his safety pilot. He was thrilled!

On the appointed day we lined up a Cessna 172 on the runway at Downtown Airport in Kansas City, Missouri. Steve was thin from cancer and bald from chemotherapy treatments, but his eyes sparkled. He pushed on the power lever for the first time in two years and we quickly rose into the air, turning west. We flew low along the Missouri river and took in the sights of the bluffs on either side. He was skilled at the controls.

Soon Steve tired, so we headed back to the airport. As we taxied to tie down the plane, I was convinced this was the most important flight I had ever made.

Each of us must know our mission. It gives us the pattern for all we do. But we must choose carefully. All our positions will one day be lost. Our possessions will deteriorate or be passed on to others. Our pleasurable experiences will fade from memory. And our projects will likely be forgotten.

Only people will last forever. Unless our highest aim in life is to love them, we're deceiving ourselves with fragile substitutes. James Dobson, psychologist and president of Focus on the Family, poetically phrased this when writing his own epitaph:

I have concluded that the accumulation of wealth, even if I could achieve it, is an insufficient reason for living. When I reach the end of my days, a moment or two from now, I must look backward on something more meaningful than the pursuit of houses and land and machines and stocks and bonds. Nor is fame of any lasting benefit. I will consider my earthly existence to have been wasted unless I can recall a loving family, a consistent investment in the lives of people, and an earnest attempt to serve the God who made me. Nothing else makes much sense."[3]

TAKE ACTION!

1) What do you believe is your mission in life? Put it into words, than tell your best friend about it.

2) Think of a way you can use one of your possessions to help someone. Make a plan and do it!

3) What's a pastime that you enjoy? How can you involve someone else in it?

CHAPTER SIX

Agape Love:
Currency of the Kingdom

Many people have trouble loving God, others, or themselves. Though it's to be our life mission, love seldom comes naturally. We must be involved in a continual process of learning how to love. Without this understanding, many of us find ourselves in situations similar to the following couple.

TRUE LOVE?

Paul and Sarah had grown very close. They began dating in college and enjoyed each other's company. As graduation approached, they became engaged and were excited by the prospect of spending the future together. Paul took a job in retail sales, working in a clothing store. He used his discount to buy nice outfits for Sarah. She began working for an accountant. In her spare time, she wrote love letters to Paul.

Paul and Sarah decided to buy a house and fix it up before their wedding. This seemed like a good idea. A house would be a sound investment, and a place they could call home. Soon they were using their spare time painting walls and fixing plumbing.

The work was more difficult and time consuming than they'd expected. Even spending every evening and weekend at their project wasn't enough! The basement had water in it. The roof leaked. The cabinets in the kitchen had rotted. The more they did, the more they found to do! And repair materials ate up all of their income.

Their relationship became strained—Sarah felt this in particular. Paul used to sit and talk with her for hours but now he just ate and ran. He didn't show her the affection he used to, either, or bring her new clothes. She began to feel lonely. Only the house and Paul's job seemed important to him now.

One night, Sarah was driving home in the snow. Her car hit a slick spot and began to spin. It slid off the road into a telephone pole. When the rescue team arrived, workers had to cut the car open to remove Sarah. Her face was smeared with blood, but she could walk. At the hospital, it was discovered her nose and jaw were broken. Soon after that, she had corrective surgery. After the surgery, Sarah was told she needed to stay in the hospital for another two weeks.

Paul came to visit her. He even brought flowers once. They talked about how to pay the medical bills and decided they might have to sell the house. When the bandages were removed, Sarah gasped in horror at her bruised and deformed face—then she wept. Paul was there, too, but he quickly left the room.

Sarah didn't hear from Paul over the next five days. *How could he ignore me at a time like this?* she wondered. Finally, she called him on the telephone.

"Paul, how are you?" she asked with some difficulty.

"Oh, I'm fine. I've been pretty busy. How about you?"

"I still have my jaw wired closed. Still, the doctor says I can leave tomorrow. Will you come get me?"

There was a long pause. Then Paul sighed. "No, Sarah. It's over."

"What do you mean, 'it's over'?" She began to tremble.

"I don't love you anymore. Our marriage is off. I've sold the house and I'm moving to Arizona."

"But you said you would always love me!" Sarah pleaded.

"I've changed my mind. I've decided you're not my type after all."

"But you *committed* yourself to me. You said nothing would ever come between us…" she sobbed. There was no reply. He'd hung up.

NO IMITATIONS!

Paul said he loved Sarah, yet his love was not the kind that could kiss an injured face. Like many of us today, Paul needed to learn how to truly love another. I believe the apostle Paul had this idea in mind when he wrote, "And this is my prayer: that your love may abound more and more in knowledge and depth of insight, so that you may be able to discern what is best and may be pure and blameless until the day of Christ" (Philippians 1:9-10).

But the term "love" can have many meanings in our culture. Some of these are:

- A strong affection for or attachment to another.
- A strong enjoyment of or interest in something (such as one's love of acting or skiing).

- An intense, usually passionate affection for a person of the opposite sex.
- The person who is the object of another person's deep affection: one's sweetheart.[1]

The ambiguous meaning of "love," unfortunately, regularly causes confusion when we try to express our feelings. In this context, we're not talking about the erotic, sensual love felt between couples, or the intimate fondness shared by friends. We're not even considering the close, even aggressive affection of parents for their children.

When Jesus spoke in Matthew 22:35-40 of loving God, others, and ourselves, He was talking about a *special* kind of love—agape. Agape love is *commitment* love. A person with agape love for another works for the welfare of that person, despite what it might cost personally.

Yet agape means more than "taking care of" another. This can be demeaning and create an unhealthy dependency in that person. Rather, loving with agape also means helping another person develop personal strengths so that the other person can better care for himself or herself. Agape love is tough and can often withstand serious assaults without faltering. This is the love we want at the foundation of our relationships. First Corinthians 13:4-7 gives us a clear picture of agape love. It can be roughly paraphrased like this:

"The person who loves another is patient and kind toward the other, and isn't jealous, boastful, or arrogant toward that person. The person who loves doesn't behave poorly or selfishly toward the loved one, neither does he or she hold a grudge against that one. The person who loves never wishes evil upon the person who is the object of that love but instead always works for the loved one's welfare."

We naturally feel closer to some people than others. But whatever kind of relationship we have, we want agape love as its foundation. Agape is the bonding agent that can best hold relationships together. Jesus Christ loves us with agape love, and has called us to do the same with those around us.

AGAPE TO YOU!

Agape love is what we want to give and receive in our relationships—it's the currency of the Kingdom of God. But upon whom should we "spend" this love? The simple mnemonic J O Y sums this up:

J Jesus
O Others
Y Yourself

The very center of our existence is built around our relationship with Jesus Christ. This relationship is not simply first but it is central to everything we are and do. We also are surrounded by many other people, who can be grouped like this:

Spouse and family members	Ephesians 5:22-33, 6:1-4
Fellow believers	Ephesians 4:1-16
Nonbelievers	1 Peter 3:15-16
People you interact with at work	Ephesians 6:5-9
The nation one is a part of	Romans 13:1-7

Some of these groups overlap. For example, if your work is that of being a student, you can relate to others as fellow students (workers) who are also believers or nonbelievers. Also, within your family some may be believers while others are nonbelievers. But for our purposes right now, let's continue to consider these five groups. J. Grant Howard illustrates our JOY-filled relationships like this:[2]

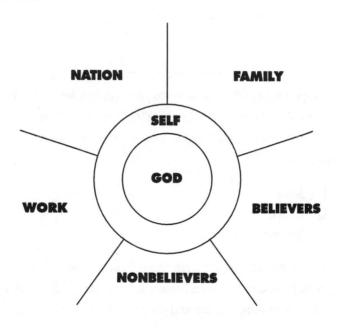

Christians in America need to have a renewed emphasis on relationships. We live in a society that stresses personal freedom, rights, mobility, wealth, and happiness. Yet our faith was never intended to be isolated from those around us. Each relationship gives us a natural context in which to express agape love, and thus to demonstrate our faith.

Our intention is to agape love our world. What do relationships based on agape love look like? Let's consider the life of the first church described in the New Testament. In Acts 2:42-47, we read:

> They devoted themselves to the apostles' teaching and to the fellowship, to the breaking of bread and to prayer. Everyone was filled with awe, and many wonders and miraculous signs were done by the apostles. All the believers were together and had everything in common. Selling their possessions and goods, they gave to anyone as he had need. Every day they continued to meet together in the temple courts. They broke bread in their homes and ate together with glad and sincere hearts, praising God and enjoying the favor of all the people. And the Lord added to their number daily those who were being saved.

Look at these people. They had a common bond—faith in Jesus Christ. When we attempt to befriend someone, it helps to have interests in common with that person. When that person isn't a believer, then we may need to look for another common interest, perhaps sports or classes. There also were common activities among the believers of Acts. To have relationships with others, we need to spend time with them and share experiences.

Mike Misko and I had undergraduate biochemistry together. I'll never forget the day I met him. I walked into class and saw this fellow sitting in the front row. He radiated friendliness. He shook my hand with a bright smile and seemed very interested in knowing me. *Surely he must be a Christian*, I thought. When I asked about this, he replied, "Of course!"

As I got to know Mike, I discovered he was just as friendly to nearly everyone he encountered. I always had a difficult time sharing my faith with professors, but Mike's warm manner won him the opportunity to share even with the associate dean of our school. Mike is a master of good relationships, and he demonstrates well the relationship principles he believes in.

The Maasai, a well-know tribe of nomadic people of eastern Africa, know the value of good relationships. When a sick person goes to a traditional Maasai healer he doesn't first ask, "How long have you been sick?" but rather, "With whom have you quarreled?" Selfishness is the biggest hindrance to good relationships (2 Timothy 3:2-5). We can't agape love until we get our minds off of ourselves. Selfishness prevents us from making wholesome commitments toward people, and it keeps us from investing the time necessary to build relationships. As we saw in the case of Paul and Sarah, where there is selfishness, little commitment, and insufficient time, it's difficult to have healthy, loving interaction.

Agape love is a high calling! It's impossible to express it consistently by our own strength; the grace of God gives us the supernatural ability to love and live this way. In 2 Corinthians 9:8, Paul tells us, "And God is able to make all grace abound to you, so that in all things at all times, having all that you need, you will abound in every good work." I like the definition of grace spoken by Paul Smith, a pastor in Kansas City, Missouri. He explained that, "Grace is God's empowering presence, enabling us to be all that He created us to be, and to do all that He has called us to do." We must rely on God's grace to agape love the people in our lives. It's too difficult to do alone.

LOVE JESUS

Loving Jesus is the first part of our mission. In this regard, 1 Peter 2:2-3 reminds us, "Like newborn babies, crave pure spiritual milk, so that by it you may grow up in your salvation, now that you have tasted that the Lord is good." The Bible is filled with details about how to love Jesus. Let's review some ways we can do this:

• *To love God we need to know His word.* It's very difficult to love a person you don't know. In 2 Timothy 3:16-17, we are reminded, "All Scripture is God-breathed and is useful for teaching, rebuking, correcting and training in righteousness, so that the man of God may be thoroughly equipped for every good work." We can know God better by reading and meditating on the Bible. Just as a couple in love continue to learn about each other, we also want to spend our lives growing ever closer to our Creator.

• *To better understand Jesus Christ we need to spend time with others who know Him.* This is one of the primary reasons churches have meetings and fellowship groups. It's also a focus of many Bible schools and seminaries, books and seminars. We need the example and leadership of mature believers. Ephesians 4:12 explains that we have the spiritual gifts in order to "prepare God's people for works of service, so that the body of Christ may be built up." But be careful. Not all who teach are teaching the truth; 1 Timothy 4:1-3 tells us some will distort it. Unfortunately, we see many examples of false teaching today.

• *To love God we must talk to Him.* Two friends will share their thoughts and feelings. The same should be true between us and God. Prayer is our opportunity to share with God. He wants to hear from us. In Matthew 6:6, Christ tells us, "When you pray, go into your room, close the door and pray to your Father, who is unseen." You see, prayer is a manifestation of our faith in God. Those who don't pray usually don't have faith. They don't see any point in it. But people who believe in God talk with Him all the time! Prayer isn't meant to be confined to a few minutes first thing in the morning—we should live in continuous communication with God. This is part of what it means to walk with Him.

I know a missionary who has had much experience sharing about Jesus with Muslims. Faithfulness in prayer is extremely important in that religious system. One day this missionary told about a church attended by a former Muslim man who had recently become a believer in Jesus Christ.

The missionary and this man were leaving a prayer meeting. The man said, "I'll see you there at noon for prayers!"

The man's enthusiasm was obvious, and the missionary was a little embarrassed. "Well, we don't meet there to pray every day, only twice a week," he replied.

"Only twice a week!" the new believer exclaimed. "How can you pray to God only twice a week? The Muslims must do so five times a day!"

By this time the missionary felt very uneasy. He silently prayed, "Lord, what can I say to this man?" Then a thought came to him. "You see, prayer is not something we do occasionally," he explained. "As Christians, we have God's Spirit within us and we can pray anytime we want [1 Thessalonians 5:17]. We don't have to be in the church building. God is always present to listen to us."

Well, this was a new idea for the man. "I thought God would only listen if I were praying in the church," he said.

"No," replied the missionary, "God wants us to pray always."

• *To show we really believe in Jesus Christ we should also want to obey Him.* Jesus said, "If you love me, you will obey what I command.... Whoever has my commands and obeys them, he is the one who loves me. He who loves me will be loved by my Father, and I too will love him and show myself to him" (John 14:15, 21). We believe Jesus' way is best and is ultimately for our own good. When we obey Him, we demonstrate that our faith and love for God are real.

Our heart attitude is vitally important. King David of ancient Israel loved God immensely. God said about David, "I have found David son of Jesse a man after my own heart; he will do everything I want him to do" (Acts 13:22). David's faith was heartfelt—not perfect, but sincere nonetheless. And he proved his faith by obeying God in some very difficult situations.

• *To love God is to be thankful.* In 1 Thessalonians 5:16-18, we are reminded to "Be joyful always; pray continually; give thanks in all circumstances, for this is God's will for you in Christ Jesus." Thankfulness to God is meant to be spontaneous and constant (Philippians 1:3). When Jesus healed the ten lepers, He wanted to know why only one of them came back to thank Him! (Luke 17:17.) As we begin to be more thankful, we will enjoy more and more the new life Jesus has given to us.

Intense military battles were fought during my first years as a medical missionary in Angola. The civil war was taking its toll, mostly among civilians. Many were hungry, frightened, sick, and separated from their families. There was talk of our town, Kalukembe, being attacked soon. I kept a backpack filled and ready for travel, should we need to evacuate. Our thoughts of attack weren't born out of paranoia. Just six months before my family and I arrived, soldiers suddenly had come running through the town, shooting at anyone they saw: women carrying their babies, old men, children. Everyone had run for their lives, hiding in the surrounding fields—even the hospital patients who were able to do so.

Urs and Ruth Beerli were Swiss medical missionaries who were trying to help these unfortunate people. With no means of escape, they and the children huddled together in the hallway of their home, away from windows. As the fighting and gunfire raged outside, they sang songs of praise to the Lord. They sang about His goodness and about how He would never leave them, no matter what. We, too, can learn to praise God regardless of our problems!

• *To love God is not an isolated activity—it involves our other relationships as well.* When we extend the hand of friendship toward others or care for our parents, we are showing love to God, too. First John 4:7-8 reminds us, "Dear friends, let us love one another, for love comes from God. Everyone who loves has been born of God and knows God. Whoever does not love does not know God, because God is love." Our love for God is vividly demonstrated by how we treat other people. Good relationships are evidence of our love for God.

The reverse is also true. If we're not right with other people, we're probably not right with God. If we act toward others with concern, respect, and agape love, this shows spiritual maturity. But if we are abusive, selfish, and bitter toward others, that suggests spiritual infancy, at best. Ultimately, if we get things right with God, He will help us get things right with others!

WHO'S MY FRIEND?

Phil, Kevin, and Curt were best friends. They had gone to the same high school, then attended college together. At college, they all were part of a student Bible study that met on campus.

One cold morning, the three of them were late and running toward class. A new library was under construction. At the site were some large earth-moving machines, and several deep trenches where the foundation was being laid. As the three trotted by, Kevin's eye caught something as it fell. He came to a stop and looked down into a huge hole in the ground. There, twenty feet below, was an elderly man lying facedown and motionless. The others had continued running. But Kevin's yell brought them right back. The three of them stared down into the pit.

"What happened to him?" Phil asked anxiously.

"He fell in," said Curt. "Look. There's a break in the fence."

"Well, let's get him out!" shouted Kevin. With one bound he was over the fence. Curt was right behind him. As they got closer to the opening, they smelled a strong odor. It was natural gas!

"We can't go down there!" shouted Kevin. "The gas could kill us! Let's call the fire department."

"That man might be dead when they get here," Curt replied.

"Phil, call for help!" Phil took off running for a phone. Kevin and Curt found a rope lying nearby. They quickly anchored one end of it to the fence. By now a crowd of students had gathered. The two lowered themselves downward, and were coughing hard when they reached the bottom.

The man was much heavier than either of them had thought he would be, and the sides of the trench were vertical. They looked at each other anxiously and made a plan. Curt tied the rope around the man's chest. Kevin then climbed up the rope to the surface above and, with the help of some bystanders, began to pull on the rope. Curt pushed from below.

Slowly they hoisted the man upward. Once topside, someone began to give him mouth to mouth resuscitation. Kevin suddenly gasped in horror to see Curt lying unconscious in the pit! He scurried down the rope again. Sirens were now audible as fire trucks neared. Kevin tied Curt's limp body to the rope and climbed the rope again. Several people helped him lift Curt to the surface. By now the firemen had arrived and they immediately began administering oxygen to the two felled by the gas. The elderly man began to breathe. Curt, however, didn't. He died later that morning.

The following week, the campus newspaper ran a front page story on the accident. Inside the paper were a number of letters to the editor dealing with the incident. Several people declared Curt had been foolish to try to save the man; Curt should have realized the danger. A philosophy major even wrote that the life of the older man was not as valuable as Curt's because the man was elderly. The predominant sentiment on campus was this: Curt should have looked out for himself!

Kevin and Phil went to their Bible study that week with heavy hearts. How surprised they were to see the man they had rescued in attendance! After the meeting was opened, the man stood up and addressed the group. "I know you all miss Curt very much. I was told he met with you." Some students looked as though they would cry. He continued, "I know Curt was your friend. Good friends are hard to come by." He had tears in his eyes. "But he was also a friend to *me*—perhaps more of a friend than I've ever had. Though I never knew him, he gave up his life for me!"

LOVE OTHERS

Loving other people sacrificially—which runs counter to human nature and popular philosophy—is the second part of our life mission. This is the theme of Christianity, and the trait for which Curt will be most remembered. We need to learn how to better love other people. Let's look at some ways to accomplish this.

• *Loving others begins at home—with your family.* Nothing reveals our character as much as the way we treat our parents, grandparents, brothers, and sisters. We can love these people by listening to their counsel. Much of what we are going through they have already experienced. They don't want to see us make the same mistakes they made! We also can love our family members by caring for their needs. This might mean mowing the lawn, washing a car, or doing the dishes. It also can include spending time talking, taking trips with family members, and even writing letters to them!

• *Show love to other believers.* When we believe in Jesus Christ, we become part of a body of believers. Jesus said, "A new commandment I give you: Love one another. As I have loved you, so you must love one another. All men will know that you are my disciples, if you love one another" (John 13:34-35). Our interaction with believers is meant to be so unique and good that other people will see us and want to believe in Jesus too!

The first step is to become part of a Bible-believing church (Hebrews 10:24-25). This requires more of us than simple membership. It means a mutual commitment with the other believers to worship God and to teach one another about our faith. It also means building friendships in which we share our struggles and pray together.

When I went off to college, I discovered a church near the campus called Cornerstone, a fellowship that had grown out of a campus ministry. I found a mix of people there: families with small children, college and professional students, and many singles. As I met with them, I realized my faith really is relevant to other adults. Cornerstone helped me apply what I believed to all parts of my life—school, dating, family relationships, even my studies.

• *Love nonbelievers.* In 2 Corinthians 5:18-20, we read that we are Jesus' ambassadors to nonbelievers on earth. How can we best love them? First, we need to point them to the One who loves them most. This isn't only the role of the pastor, evangelist, or missionary. We're *all* called to tell the people in our personal world about Jesus (1 Peter 3:15-16). Each of us knows nonbelievers—such as roommates, neighbors, classmates, or colleagues at work. We may be the only Christian friends or acquaintances these people have. Who else will tell them about Jesus Christ? Our opportunities are unlimited!

Another important way to love nonbelievers is by meeting their physical and emotional needs. Our words are important, but they need to be backed up by demonstrations of love (Ephesians 2:10). We can give clothes and food to shelters, financially sponsor needy children, or provide rides or run errands for the elderly. Through service we can gain the privilege of sharing our faith.

• *Love those you meet through your employment.* Work is a fact of life (2 Thessalonians 3:10-12). Most of us spend the best hours of our days and best days of our lives at work. How can we agape love people in a work environment? Perhaps the most important way is to have an excellent attitude, doing our job to the best of our ability. This is true of our schooling and studies, as well as in formal employment settings. Does this sound like a revolutionary idea? It is!

Opportunities to speak for Jesus Christ can spring naturally from our work when it's done with unusual quality. This shouldn't be hard for us to do, for it's ultimately not our employer we serve, or even ourselves, but Jesus Christ: "And whatever you do, whether in word or deed, do it all in the name of the Lord Jesus, giving thanks to God the Father through him" (Colossians 3:17). We are Jesus' representatives, even on the job!

Jim was a young man who worked to put himself through college at a golf club. He had been doing his best to be on time, be friendly to customers, and keep his accounts straight. His manager was skeptical of him, though. Their relationship became strained. One day they were talking behind the counter. "You know, I think you want my job," said the manager.

"Why in the world would you think that?" Jim replied, stunned.

"Because you're always trying so hard to please everyone here. The owner is going to think you're a better man for the job than me." He was serious.

Jim shook his head in disbelief. "No, that's not true," he said. "I'm a Christian, and I'm working here to help make you successful."

Now the manager was stunned. "I've never heard anything like that in my life. You're working to make *me* successful? Nobody does that!"

"But it's true!" my friend continued. "It's part of my calling as a Christian."

"This is incredible...but I'll think about it," the manager said as he walked away. From that time on, their relationship took on a freshness. And later, Jim was able to share about Jesus Christ with his manager.

We live in a very self-seeking world. The one who works with a good attitude can make a remarkable impression on those around him or her!

• *Love your country*. All Christians are also part of a nation and must interact with their government. How can we love our nation? One way is to make wise decisions regarding elections, courts, taxes, and military service. We also need to be a voice for justice on social issues. And as much as possible, we should obey our authorities (Romans 13:1-4) and pray for them. The apostle Paul said, "I urge, then, first of all, that requests, prayers, intercession and thanksgiving be made for everyone—for kings and all those in authority, that we may live peaceful and quiet lives in all godliness and holiness. This is good, and pleases God our Savior" (1 Timothy 2:1-3).

Truly, learning the countless ways to love others is a never-ending process, with room for unlimited creativity! Of all the education we can possibly receive, this is some of the most essential.

SUPER GAIL

Gail was a popular freshman. She was part of the church prayer team and the refreshment committee. Gail even visited the women's prison. She never missed a church meeting and usually brought friends. But that wasn't all. Gail also was on the women's basketball team at her college, and class secretary!

Gail was so energetic and involved, her friends thought she could do almost anything. If there was an incomplete project, they would say, "Ask Gail!" If someone needed help with his or her studies, they would look her up. Even in the middle of the night she always provided a concerned, listening ear for anyone who came by.

But all this activity began to wear on Gail. By Christmas break she looked haggard. When she arrived home for the holidays, Gail visited her best friend, Kathy, who had gone to a different college. Kathy asked Gail how she was feeling.

"Just fine. I really like college," replied Gail.

But Kathy was concerned. "Then why did I find you asleep on my living room floor this morning?"

"Oh, I'm just a little tired, that's all. I'm going to the library to work on a paper now." She began to pick up her books.

"Why now? You're on break!"

"I didn't get it done on time, so the professor said I could do the paper over vacation. Bye, Kathy—got to run!"

When school started again, Gail plunged back into her activities. She enjoyed helping people. She also was taking nineteen credit hours! Her stomach began to ache often, but she didn't visit the doctor at the campus health center. She really didn't think she could afford to take the time.

One day after drill team practice she began to feel nauseated. Gail ran to the locker room and had the shock of her life when she began to vomit blood! An ambulance rushed her to a hospital. She was in intensive care and needed blood transfusions. The doctor said she suffered from a bleeding ulcer.

A few days later, the bleeding stopped. Kathy was there, and she and Gail were talking.

"The doctor says I need to take it easy," sighed Gail. "He wants me to cut back on my activities."

"What do *you* think about that?" her friend replied, trying not to sound judgmental.

"Well, I wonder who would serve the refreshments this week? I'm also supposed to lead Sunday School. I can't let everyone down!"

Kathy shook her head. "But Gail, what if you had died?" She brushed away a tear.

There was a long silence. "You're right," Gail said thoughtfully. "I'm going to have to say no to some things. I've got to take care of myself. Otherwise, I won't be any good to anybody!"

IS IT OK TO LOVE YOURSELF?

We live in a very self-centered world. On the other hand, the Bible says we Christians are radically different people who are willing to care for others above ourselves. So, is there any room for us to love *ourselves*?

Matthew 22:39 reminds us to "Love your neighbor as yourself." Notice that Jesus isn't saying in this passage to "Love your neighbor *in place of* yourself." I'm convinced Jesus says to love our neighbors as ourselves because He is aware that self-love, in proper perspective, is essential and elementary to loving others. If you have healthy self-love and self-acceptance, you can serve God better, accept other people, exercise responsibility, be emotionally expressive, and flexible. You also can better accept rebuke, insult, and criticism. You will perform at your maximum ability!

In his book *Dr. Dobson Answers Your Questions*, the noted Christian psychologist writes of a question that was addressed to him: "You are strongly in favor of building self-esteem in children, but I have some theological problems with that objective. The Bible condemns 'pride' from Genesis to Revelation, and speaks of humans as no better than worms. How do you defend your position in the light of Scripture?"

Dr. Dobson replied:

It is my opinion that great confusion has prevailed among followers of Christ on the distinction between pride and self-esteem. You are apparently among the people who actually believe that Christians should maintain an attitude of inferiority in order to avoid the pitfalls of self-sufficiency and haughtiness. I don't believe it.

After speaking to a sizable audience in Boston a few years ago, I was approached by an elderly lady who questioned my views. I had discussed the importance of self-confidence in children, and my comments had contradicted her theology. In fact, she even made reference to the same Scripture, Psalm 22:6.

She said, "God wants me to think of myself as being no better than a worm. I would like to respect myself," she continued, "but God could not approve of that kind of pride, could he?"

I was touched as this sincere little lady spoke. She told me she had been a missionary for forty years, even refusing to marry in order to serve God more completely. While on a foreign field, she had become ill with an exotic disease which now reduced her frail body to ninety-five pounds. As she spoke, I could sense the great love of the Heavenly Father for this faithful servant. She had literally given her life in his work, yet she did not even feel entitled to reflect on a job well done during her closing years on earth.

Unfortunately, this fragile missionary (and thousands of others Christians) had been taught that she was worthless. But that teaching did not come from the Scriptures. Jesus did not leave his throne in heaven to die for the "worms" of the world. His sacrifice was intended for that little woman, and for me and all of his followers, whom he is not embarrassed to call brothers. What a concept! If Jesus in now my brother, then that puts me in the family of God, and guarantees that I will outlive the universe itself. And that, friends, is what I call genuine self-esteem![3]

The third part of our mission in life is to love ourselves. But selfishness is wrong. We need to have a healthy, balanced view of who we really are. I believe Paul had this idea in mind when he wrote, "For by the grace given me I say to every one of you: Do not think of yourself more highly than you ought, but rather think of yourself with sober judgment, in accordance with the measure of faith God has given you" (Romans 12:3).

Each of us must decide how to meet our personal needs in the context of the needs of others. Some believers need to take the focus off themselves and turn their attention toward others. Others need to take better care of themselves and stop neglecting their personal needs. This self/others tension is one every sincere Christian experiences. Loving ourselves shouldn't necessarily be equated with selfishness. Rather, it's an essential part of loving God, who created us, and loving others, whom we can best serve if we are healthy ourselves.

WHAT ARE YOUR LEGITIMATE NEEDS?

God created us with some basic legitimate needs. In fact, we're very needy creatures, requiring food, shelter, companionship, rest, and recreation. If we don't have these things, we risk fatigue, inefficiency, depression, and illness. Gail fell into this trap. In an overstretched condition like hers, it's almost impossible to serve others.

We can learn something about our personal needs by looking at Luke 2:52—"And Jesus grew in wisdom and stature, and in favor with God and men." Like you and I, Christ had spiritual, social, mental, and physical attributes. Corresponding to each of these attributes are legitimate personal needs. Dick Couey, an exercise physiologist from Baylor University and former professional baseball player, emphasizes this fact in his book, *Happiness Is Being a Physically Fit Christian*.[4] Our legitimate personal needs include:

• *Spiritual needs.* Micah 6:8 explains, "He has showed you, O man, what is good. And what does the Lord require of you? To act justly and to love mercy and to walk humbly with your God." As we learn to love God and develop our relationship with him, our spiritual needs begin to be met. A healthy spiritual life then becomes the basis for our social, mental, and physical development.

• *Social needs.* People were never meant to be isolated from one another. All of us need support, advice, and nurturing. As we learn to love others, people often respond by helping us meet our own social and intimacy needs. This is an exchange, but we must take the initiative!

• *Mental/emotional needs.* We all have thoughts and experience emotions. We respond to situations by feeling angry, mischievous, sad, or happy. This variety adds unique flavor to our lives. Why is God concerned about what we think? Because outward behavior is an expression of what is on the inside. Philippians 4:8 tells us, "Finally, brothers, whatever is true, whatever is noble, whatever is right, whatever is pure, whatever is lovely, whatever is admirable—if anything is excellent or praiseworthy—think about such things." We must consciously decide to focus on Christ-oriented thoughts and feelings that can change and revitalize us.

• *Physical needs.* God reminds us in 1 Corinthians 6:19-20, "Do you not know that your body is a temple of the Holy Spirit, who is in you, whom you have received from God? You are not your own; you were bought at a price. Therefore honor God with your body." Our bodies belong to Jesus Christ, and when we take care of our health we honor Him! A simple strategy for maintaining physical health can be summarized with the easy-to-remember mnemonic formula, H E A L T H:

HEALTH   Hygiene—practice it!

HEALTH   Exercise!

HEALTH   Eat right!

HEALTH   Alcohol, tobacco, and other

              drugs—No!

HEALTH   Accidents—prevent them!

HEALTH   Lust—control it!

HEALTH   Time out—reduce stress!

HEALTH   Help from your physician—

              when you need it, get it!

Many things are exchanged between individuals in our world: cash, cars, houses, knowledge, status, and so on. But the most important commodity is also the most difficult to find—agape love. Our mission is to freely distribute this treasure to the people around us. It's not an easy task, and we must always be learning how to better handle this currency of God's Kingdom.

TAKE ACTION!

1) What can you do to show God you love him? List three things.

2) What can you do today to show your appreciation of your parents?

3) Are you truly committed to a church? What can you do to build your relationship with those believers?

4) Who are two nonbelievers you know? How can you share the Good News with them?

5) How can you do your work or studies better? Do you need to change your attitude?

6) Are you praying for your nation's leaders? If not, will you begin today? List some specific leaders who need your prayers.

7) What do you need to do to take better care of yourself? For example, do you need more exercise? Make a list.

PART THREE

OUR
STRATEGY:

*Built with
Wisdom*

Popcorn Decisions

When we trust Jesus to lead us and we understand our mission in life, we have a solid foundation upon which to make good decisions. I believe Paul had this in mind when he wrote in 1 Corinthians 3:10-13:

By the grace God has given me, I laid a foundation as an expert builder, and someone else is building on it. But each one should be careful how he builds. For no one can lay any foundation other than the one already laid, which is Jesus Christ. If any man builds on this foundation using gold, silver, costly stones, wood, hay, or straw, his work will be shown for what it is, because the Day will bring it to light. It will be revealed with fire, and the fire will test the quality of each man's work.

We need to have a clear foundation for making specific life decisions. Yet these basics—our trust in Jesus and an understanding of our life mission as a Christian—are omitted in most discussions of planning or personal management. Is it any wonder, then, that so many people do a good job of deciding on the wrong things? Even as we begin to look at making specific choices, we must keep our focus on our Leader and our overall mission as a believer.

Before you make a specific decision, be certain you fully understand the issue in question. What exactly needs to be decided? Write out the issue as clearly as possible on a piece of paper. Sometimes there really is more than one question to be considered. For example, decisions about career choice and college selection are often lumped together. We might do better by dealing with them separately.

MAJOR EARTHQUAKES

Some decisions have major consequences, while the outcome of others will be more minor. Of course, what people consider to be major or minor may vary, but the distinction is still helpful. Major decisions are those involving greater responsibility, work, and/or commitment. The more important the implications, the more careful you will need to be! Some major decisions may include:

Relating to JESUS:

—Will I believe in Jesus Christ as my Savior and Leader?

—Will I continue to believe even though I'm rejected by my friends?

Relating to OTHERS:

Family:

—Should I live near my parents?

—Whom shall I marry?

Believers:

—What church should I join?

—Should I start a youth group at church?

Nonbelievers:

—Shall I start a Bible study in the dorm?

—What can I do to show Jesus' love to Carol?

People at work:

—Where should I go to college?

—Where should I work after graduation?

The nation:

—Should I join the military?

—For whom shall I vote for president?

Relating to YOURSELF:

—Where should I live?

—Shall I buy a car now?

MINOR TREMORS

Minor decisions are ones that involve less commitment and have fewer consequences. But minor decisions are still important, for our major decisions can usually only be accomplished through the minor ones which follow. It's often the seemingly unimportant steps that determine whether we'll be successful.

For example, a person decides to learn to play a musical

instrument. After this, many smaller decisions must follow: which instructor to hire, where to practice, whether to buy an instrument or rent one, what music to perform, and so on. Similarly, a couple decides to become engaged. Then they must begin to work through lesser decisions about their wedding, honeymoon, and first home. Some of these may turn out to be more significant than the couple imagined, so these decisions also need to be made carefully. Some minor decisions include:

Relating to JESUS:

    —When should I have my quiet time today?

    —Shall I pray about the anxiety I'm feeling?

Relating to OTHERS:
    Family:

    —Should I visit my parents this weekend?

    —Shall I go on this canoe trip with my brother?
    Believers:

    —Whom should I date this weekend?

    —Shall I go to worship on Sunday?
    Nonbelievers:

    —How can I tell Fred about my faith during lunch tomorrow?

    —Shall I say hello to the new person in my chemistry class?

People at work:

—When should I study?

—Can I afford to be a few minutes late for work today?

The nation:

—Should I drive over the speed limit?

—Who will prepare my taxes?

Relating to YOURSELF:

—What should I wear today?

—What shall I eat for breakfast?

WHAT WE NEED IS...

The preceding lists include examples of specific choices we make to fulfill our mission in life. We're free to make most individual decisions, as long as we stay within the general guidelines of God's will. But even then we aren't without resources to help us decide. God has offered us *wisdom.* This is an important theme of the Bible, and a key tool in successful decision-making. By wisdom, I mean, "good judgment, based on knowledge; discretion."[1] Dr. J.I. Packer's definition of wisdom is better yet: "Wisdom is the power to see, and the inclination to choose, the best and highest goal, together with the surest means of attaining it."[2] It's the ability to accurately assess a situation and then decide what is best to do.

As a young adult I made my first major decisions very intuitively. Rather than carefully consider the implications of my actions, I tended to follow my feelings alone. It isn't surprising that I was often burned in the process! Following one's intuition is not all wrong, but I desperately needed the help of wisdom.

Wisdom is a precious thing—more valuable than money or prestige. Proverbs 3:13-14 tells us, "Blessed is the man who finds wisdom, the man who gains understanding, for she is more profitable than silver and yields better returns than gold." Wisdom will help keep us from evil and preserve our lives (Proverbs 5:1-2; Ecclesiastes 7:11-12). It is one of our best defenses against life's problems! (Ecclesiastes 9:18.)

So, where can we obtain wisdom? It comes from God—the Creator of wisdom. He wants to give us wisdom, but we must *seek* it. The Old Testament puts it this way, "...if you call out for insight and cry aloud for understanding, and if you look for it as for silver and search for it as for hidden treasure, then you will understand the fear of the LORD and find the knowledge of God. For the LORD gives wisdom, and from his mouth come knowledge and understanding" (Proverbs 2:3-6). The New Testament says, "If any of you lacks wisdom, he should ask God, who gives generously to all without finding fault, and it will be given to him. But when he asks, he must believe and not doubt, because he who doubts is like a wave of the sea, blown and tossed by the wind" (James 1:5-6).

Perhaps the greatest obstacle to gaining or understanding wisdom is evil in our lives. Evil will warp our judgment. Of course, we never reach perfection in this lifetime. As Christians we may be more conscious of sin that ever before, and perhaps better able to avoid its snare. But we need to take an honest look inside ourselves and determine if there is any overt sin that should be acknowledged and dealt with before we attempt to make important decisions. A clear conscience before God is at the heart of understanding how to live (Acts 24:16; 2 Corinthians 4:1-2).

King Solomon was known for his great wisdom. As a young man he became ruler of ancient Israel—an awesome responsibility for which he was unprepared. So, Solomon asked God for wisdom instead of anything else (1 Kings 3). Wisdom was more important to Solomon than material possessions, physical health, or political victories. In response to his honest request, God gave him more wisdom than any other person of his time, and his leadership in Israel was unsurpassed.

Like Solomon, we also need wisdom to decide what to do in each situation that confronts us (Ephesians 5:15-16; Colossians 4:5). To make wise decisions about career, marriage, and almost anything else, we must like POPCORN! Much biblical teaching concerning wise decision-making can be summed up in this mnemonic.

POPCORN GUIDELINES
FOR DECISION-MAKING

P	Pray for wisdom.
O	List the Options.
P	Weigh the Pros.
C	Weigh the Cons.
O	Open your Bible.
R	Get Recommendations.
N	No hurry!

PRAY FOR WISDOM

The first step in making a good decision is to pray for wisdom (James 1:5-6; Colossians 1:9-10). Share with God your feelings and thoughts about the issue in question. Then ask him for his help in making the decision. Praying like this lets God know you trust him. It also will remind you you're not alone in the decision-making process. God has promised to help.

Peace is one benefit we receive from prayer. Philippians 4:6-7 tells us, "Do not be anxious about anything, but in everything, by prayer and petition, with thanksgiving, present your requests to God. And the peace of God, which transcends all understanding, will guard your hearts and your minds in Christ Jesus." We can relax more when we trust him with our questions.

As I was about to graduate from medical school, I was faced with a tough choice. Where should I work? There were many options, but they seemed so hard to evaluate. Most of my friends made selections without any trouble, but my anxiety only grew as the application deadlines grew closer.

One day I was sharing my struggles with a friend, Carl Werner. "Have you prayed about it?" he asked. "Of course!" was my desperate reply. Carl looked at me, perplexed. "Then why don't you trust God and stop worrying?" Carl had identified my problem exactly. I let out a sigh. Anxiety had clouded my judgment. Only when I began to trust God to help me was I able to gather my thoughts and make a confident choice.

LIST THE OPTIONS

Next, write down all possible answers, solutions, or options that come to mind. Have a brain-storming session in which you sit down and let your imagination go! If possible, ask others to help you. Solutions often come to us only after we give up our preconceived notions and think freely of creative or unusual alternatives. Don't be too hasty to eliminate any ideas.

For example, biology majors such as myself often have difficulty finding work in their field. One classmate of mine dreamed of several possibilities, including teaching junior high school, being a research assistant, or managing a city zoo. However, the more she thought about employment, the more anxious she became. My friend prematurely concluded she could never find work in biology, so she settled for a full-time waitress job after graduation. If she had done some investigating, though, she'd have found that a local research firm was looking for employees with her training. Several of our friends signed on with this firm. But her unwillingness to fully consider the options proved to be a major setback to her career.

Let me give you a personal example. Halfway through college, the car I drove finally gave out. I sold it, along with a camper, and had one thousand dollars with which to buy another car. I longed for a fast muscle car like several friends owned. I also liked the sleek luxury autos of my wealthier classmates. But I had so little money, how could I afford to buy, let alone maintain, such a car?

I struggled with this dilemma for weeks, when one day I had a new idea. Why not simply swallow my pride and buy a low-maintenance, low-budget car that would not eat up my bank account? The idea grew on me. I bought such a car and drove it, trouble-free, for twelve years. But I might have missed this terrific plan if I hadn't given up some of my notions of what a car should be, and let in a new perspective.

WEIGH THE PROS AND CONS

Almost every option has advantages and disadvantages. We need to know what these are in advance. The sooner we see the implications of a particular choice, the sooner we'll make better decisions. Spencer Johnson, author of *The One Minute Manager*, put it like this: "Our poor decisions were based on illusions we believed at the time, and our better decisions on realities we recognized in time."[3]

Gather as much information as possible about your options from books, conferences, videos, magazine articles, and so on. Then go through each of them, visualizing yourself in those potential situations. Begin writing a list of the corresponding pros and cons. First, consider your abilities and limitations. Each of us has certain skills, interests, spiritual gifts, supplies, time, and money. Do you have the resources necessary for each option? Be honest with yourself. Generally, it's better to operate in the area of your strengths.

Also consider your responsibilities and relationships. How will a potential decision affect your interaction with Jesus, your family, church, nonbelievers, work, the nation, and how will it affect *you*? Most decisions can't be made in a vacuum. For example, if you decide to take a job in another city and move away, your present responsibilities and most of your relationships will be drastically affected!

Jesus mentioned the importance of considering the pros and cons. In Luke 14:28-30, He says, "Suppose one of you wants to build a tower. Will he not first sit down and estimate the cost to see if he has enough money to complete it? For if he lays the foundation and is not able to finish it, everyone who sees it will ridicule him, saying, 'This fellow began to build and was not able to finish.' " It takes effort to think through the implications of each option, but if you do, your decisions will be greatly improved!

OPEN YOUR BIBLE

Next, check the Bible to locate any specific instructions concerning your decision. For example, you might be single and feeling a lot of sexual frustration. How should you handle this? First Corinthians 6:18-20 yields some important counsel. Or you might be considering whether or not to join a Christian fellowship. Hebrews 10:24-5 has some good information for you to consider before making this decision.

When there's no specific instruction given, look for a principle that applies. For example, you might have a free weekend. What should you do? Your options might be either to go fishing or to work at a camp for the handicapped. The Bible doesn't give any specific instructions for this situation, but Philippians 2:3-4 advises us to put the welfare of others before ourselves, and Mark 6:31 points out the importance of personal rest. These principles may help you weigh your decision.

GET RECOMMENDATIONS

We can always find people who know more than we do. Asking for their advice isn't a sign of weakness but is instead evidence of wisdom. Proverbs 15:22 tells us, "Plans fail for lack of counsel, but with many advisers they succeed." Proverbs 19:20 urges, "Listen to advice and accept instruction, and in the end you will be wise." By setting aside our ego and listening to the counsel of others, we often can avoid many pitfalls (Proverbs 11:14, 12:15, 13:20, 20:18, 24:6). It takes time to set up appointments and get advice from others. But the investment usually pays off well.

It's especially important to talk with people to whom we are responsible. These could include our parents, girlfriend or boyfriend, employer, and pastor. To ask their advice is a way of honoring these people. It says, "You are important and I can learn from you." It also helps to enlist their support, which can be very important later on if you encounter problems and need help.

In particular, ask your parents for their opinions. Proverbs 6:20 says, "My son, keep your father's commands and do not forsake your mother's teaching." While you may be beyond their legal authority, it's still wise to seek your parents' input, for they probably know you better than anyone else. As I considered working in Angola, I had a talk with my father. The decision would have a big impact on him. My father wouldn't see me or his grandchildren for three or four years. He explained that he would really miss us, and asked if we couldn't try to stay closer. I understood his feelings. It would be hard to be separated. Though we did move to Angola, my father still knows we thought enough of him to ask for his advice.

<u>N</u>O HURRY!

Good decisions demand hard work, concentration, and time. Generally, the more time and energy we spend, the better the outcome will be. We also will feel more content about these decisions. Emotionally-charged decisions, like those surrounding marriage or major purchases, particularly call for unhurried evaluation, to help you sort out the truth.

Proverbs 21:5 reminds us that "The plans of the diligent lead to profit as surely as haste leads to poverty." Fast, impulsive decisions can be the most regrettable. When you are in a hurry, there's usually not enough time to consider all the factors and implications involved in a particular decision. Taking sufficient time, however, allows us to test and probe the options, revealing perspectives that fast action overlooks.

Begin considering your choices as early as possible so you won't be rushed. Try to go slowly and keep your options open as long as you can. Major decisions should be made at a time when you feel rested and can focus your attention on them. If possible, take several days off to relax and clear your mind; then work through your decision. When we give decisions enough time, confusion tends to dissipate and our choices often become more straightforward.

DECIDE!

There are several important guidelines for making wise decisions, and it's a good idea to employ as many as you can. When an airplane is flying, the pilot doesn't rely upon any single method of navigation alone—it may be faulty. Instead, he prefers to use several different ways to navigate: the compass and clock, radio beacons, landmarks, and others. The captain checks them against one another to be sure he's staying on course. In the same way, we can't rely upon just one or two guidelines for decision-making. We need several to be certain we're going in the best direction. The more important the decision, the more care we need to take.

Many people fail to make choices because they are looking for a perfect option—one that is all good. We too often forget that even with the best decisions there usually will be some potentially negative outcome to consider. Most decisions are not absolutely right or wrong. If they were, they might be easier to make. We are more often confronted with gray areas that come with numerous pros and cons on either side of the ledger. In these situations, try to make decisions that lead to maximum good, and minimum problems.

Our decisions should bring us a sense of peace or contentment. In 1 Corinthians 14:33, we read that ours is a God of peace. Likewise, peace is one of the fruits of the work of the Holy Spirit in our lives (Galatians 5:22), and is an attribute which should characterize all Christians. With regard to decision-making, peace often is an inner signal that we have come to a resolution or consensus. This is consistent with our understanding of truth. It's good to remember, though, that some anxiety surrounding any big decision is normal: Experiencing cold, clammy hands before one's wedding, for example, can often be expected. But persistent overall contentment about a decision is an important factor to look for.

The opposite of peace is doubt. Decisions should be acts of faith and confidence, not symptoms of confusion. When we are unsettled, we shouldn't commit ourselves yet. Instead, we need to wait and keep our options open as long as possible. We also need to pray, ask for wisdom, and continue to carefully evaluate the situation before making a choice.

Some decisions require more than contentment and acceptability. Those concerning marriage and career fall into this group. They demand true conviction and determination. Ambivalence will not do. We know beforehand that such decisions will involve long-term commitment and real challenges. It's when the going gets tough that we need the conviction that we really worked at making wise choices in the first place.

WHAT CAREER?

I began to think about my career choice when I was a senior in high school. It was hard for me to consider such a major decision at that time. I preferred simply to do my homework, run track, and play my trombone. Still, I knew I needed to put aside some of my activities and think about the future. High school was not going to last forever.

First I prayed about this matter. I was part of a Christian fellowship at school, and many students in our group were faced with similar decisions. So when we met Tuesday mornings before class, we prayed as a group for insight. I wasn't alone in my searching for answers; I had the support of the Lord and my friends. Knowing this helped a lot!

It's important that we don't make decisions simply to please others: Be fully convinced of the rightness of a decision in your own mind. We need to listen to the counsel of others, but at some point we must stop and decide autonomously—for ourselves. Otherwise, we will find ourselves feeling manipulated and suppressed, or missing out on the full joy that making good decisions can bring! I had to keep this in mind while I considered my future career.

I listed different careers I could choose. As the weeks went by, the list grew longer and longer, for my interests were broad. I considered being a classical musician, an airline pilot, an electronics engineer, and going into business with my father. I was interested in so many areas, it was hard to sort through them. So I began to weigh the pros and cons of each: educational requirements, job security and competition, my personal interest, salary potential, and how much free time each would provide. My list looked something like this:

MY CAREER CHOICES
(KEY: 0 = BAD; 1 = GOOD)

Career	Education	Security	Interest	Salary	Free time	TOTALS
Musician	1	0	1	0	1	3
Pilot	1	0	1	1	1	4
Engineer	0	1	1	0	0	2
Business	1	0	0	1	0	2
Medicine	0	1	1	1	0	3

Next, I looked in the Bible for advice. I knew I was responsible to care for myself and my future family (2 Thessalonians 3:10). I also wanted to do my work well (Colossians 3:23-24). But I didn't find any specific instructions about which career to choose. I felt undecided, and the deadlines for college application were coming up quickly. What helped at that point was some good counsel. I talked with some teachers about my options. I even found a professional musician, a pilot, and an engineer to interview. But what helped most was talking to my parents. They gave me new perspectives, and were the first to recommend that I go into medicine. I had never thought seriously of that option before.

I applied to various college programs and continued to pray with the group at school. The months of waiting for replies gave me more time to think through my options. I had a growing conviction that a career in medicine would be good for me, and in the spring of 1976 I received a letter of acceptance. Though I've had struggles in my career, I've never regretted my choice.

WHICH COMPANION?

POPCORN guidelines don't apply only to rather impersonal choices, such as one's career or car selection. These same guidelines can also help guide our most intimate relationships, as I saw in the situation of Steve and Krystal. I met this couple at a decision-making seminar I gave one spring.

They prayed for months about their future together, asking God to give them the ability to make a good choice. Fortunately, there was enough trust between Steve and Krystal that they were able to talk openly about their strengths and weaknesses, both as individuals and as a couple. The more they did this, the better the two could see how their marriage might be. For example, Steve's parents were divorced, and Krystal anticipated the difficulty of dealing with two sets of in-laws. But Steve was so kind to them all—a trait she admired.

Krystal, on the other hand, had a graduate degree and a good job, while Steve never graduated from college and had a hard time finding more than minimum-wage work. He felt a little intimidated by her, professionally and intellectually. But despite this, Steve appreciated the way she thoughtfully managed her money.

Sometimes they talked about faith. After reading 2 Corinthians 6:14, Steve felt strongly that he wanted a wife who believed much the way he did. But Krystal and he disagreed over many spiritual issues, leading to growing tension.

Over the spring, the couple had time to talk with their friends and parents, who were usually eager to say what they thought of Steve and Krystal's potential together.

"Steve," Krystal said after a movie one evening, "I've been thinking a lot about us...*you* know, over the long run." The young man sighed, as if relieved she'd brought it up. "Yes, I have, too."

"I really like you," she said with sincerity. "But we're so different. Maybe we should start dating others." Krystal now had a tear in her eye.

There was a silent pause. Steve began to feel a little choked up, but spoke with conviction. "I think you're right." Another pause followed as he reached for her hand. "But I'll miss you!"

Steve and Krystal used remarkable wisdom to see the limitations of their relationship, and were courageous enough to take the next step, in spite of the inevitable heartache. But months later, after some of the emotions had subsided, they each told me independently that this was one of their best decisions ever.

THE GREAT MATE DEBATE

Our marriage decisions are usually the most far-reaching of any we make in our lives. Each year millions of people plan their futures together—some for better and many for worse. In evaluating our dating relationships, we may ask questions like: "Do we respect each other?" "Can we make it financially?" "What do our friends think of our relationship?"

These are good questions, and they can help us realize when engagement is right. But none of them alone gets to the heart of what most of us want marriage to be. Because we don't ask the best questions, many people get into relationships that maybe never should have started.

I believe the most important question—the one which best gets at the essence of marriage—is, "Can our relationship create a lifetime of intimacy, passion, and mutual help?" Let's break this question down into its parts to get a better look.

Can... Up front, we're trying to make a prediction. We're forecasting the way things may be. For most of us, this doesn't come easily. Decision-making is a skill, like playing basketball or driving a car. We must concentrate and practice to become good at it. Don't let your engagement decision be the first major decision you ever make. First, develop your decision-making skills with choices that are less important, like selecting a college, career, or church.

...our relationship create... Relationships rarely come without effort. They're built by people who can be innovative and are willing to give 100 percent, even if the other doesn't reciprocate. Sound like a high calling? It is. And, unfortunately, many marriages go poorly because couples can't (or won't) invest unselfishly

in the relationship. Yet when two people do show this kind of commitment, they're the envy of the world!

...a lifetime... In the course of our lives, we make few commitments that are meant to last forever—for the demands of these promises are great. Yet within the security of our covenant with our mate lies the potential for enormous warmth, growth, and joy. Marriage is worth working long and hard to guard.

Tony and Gail felt this way when they talked with me, just before graduation, about their engagement. But after a few months, Gail began to doubt she was ready for so much commitment. She doubted that Tony was either, so they put off their plans. If lifetime dedication is an idea that scares you, then, like Gail and Tony, don't marry yet!

...of intimacy... This is the ability to trust, confide in, listen to, comfort, counsel, and nurture each other. In short, it's companionship in its deepest form. Intimacy is always easier when things are going well between two people. But how do the two of you deal with conflict? This is a good way to see just how close you really are. Conflict is inevitable. If you can deal with it in an open, constructive manner, this says a lot for the strength of your relationship! On the other hand, if you can't handle conflict, be careful about engagement. And if you haven't had any strong disagreements, you haven't been dating long enough!

...passion... The sensual part of marriage can be wonderful, particularly in contrast with all of today's sexual abuses. Sexual attraction is meant to be a fun, encouraging component of marriage.

We naturally want to choose partners we're attracted to. But watch out for infatuation. While these exciting feelings are enjoyable, they can keep us from appreciating one another's more important qualities. Don't be satisfied with just a passing notion of delight, but look for enduring inner beauty in your potential mate.

...*and mutual help?* Marriage is partnership in its purest sense—two people working together, hand in hand, side by side. Are the two of you going the same direction in life? Do your plans agree? Are you willing to help each other—even sacrifice—to accomplish them? To what extent, and for how long?

Perhaps the most important function of the wedding ring is not simply to remind the world of one's vows, but to test the commitment of the purchaser—usually the man. If he's willing to part with several weeks' or even months' wages for the woman he loves, he's showing a degree of commitment. In the same way, test your commitment to each other in practical ways before making a pact for life.

The best way to predict if your relationship has marriage potential is to gain experience together developing and affirming the qualities you desire in one another. When relationships begin, we tend to be on our best behavior, and are often willing to overlook unattractive traits in our prospective mate. Over time, though, couples become more "real" to each other. And since few of us suddenly change much in personality or interaction when we become married, we usually can recognize what we're getting into before the wedding day. For these reasons, many counselors recommend that a couple date at least two years before deciding to marry.

As you approach a marriage decision, also consider whether you're becoming engaged primarily because your relationship measures up, or because you don't want to be alone. Personal insecurity sometimes causes us to compromise our decisions with the thought, "I'd better settle for this companion; I may not get another chance at marriage." Yet the worst loneliness is usually still better than a bad marriage.

If your relationship makes the mark—if your intimacy, passion, and commitment stand the test of time—you may well have found your mate! If not, don't become engaged, at least not yet. Don't compromise when selecting your marriage partner.

No relationship is perfect, but you can dramatically increase the quality of your marriage by asking the right question, and not becoming engaged until you both can give an honest and resounding "Yes!"

WHAT IF YOU MAKE A MISTAKE?

Despite great care, you may later think you made a wrong choice concerning any number of relationships. This can cause terrible anguish, hopelessness, anger, denial, and depression. What can we do in these situations?

On the positive side, remember that making mistakes is part of being human; no one is perfect. We can learn from our errors how to make better decisions in the future. And our own mistakes can help us be less judgmental when other people blow it, and make it easier for us to forgive the shortcomings of our friends.

Mistakes can help teach us, or enable us to better appreciate, some essential spiritual truths. Our fragility, dependence on God, and the reality of his compassion often become more apparent. The seriousness of sin and its consequences may become more real, too. I must add that not all mistakes are the result of sin.

Often we err in nonmoral ways, such as when we buy an inappropriate car. When sin is involved, forgiveness and grace are concepts that can come alive in the midst of our failures—particularly helping us learn to forgive ourselves. And with mistakes can come a sense of peace that surpasses our understanding and helps us rise above our anxiety-producing circumstances.

Some commitments aren't absolute. If you find yourself going down the wrong road and can turn around, do it! Don't let pride, your track record, or fears of what others may think keep you from confronting the problem. The popular idea that Christians don't, or shouldn't, have serious personal problems is a dangerous myth which can keep us from dealing with our conflicts. Don't simply get involved in some other activity to take your mind off a troublesome issue. Pray about the matter, get some advice, and see if you have an option of escape.

If you can't change course, remember that God can make positive use of our mistakes (Romans 8:28). Learn to deal with your feelings. Don't let an error cripple your outlook on life! Remember the apostle Paul's situation: He had bitterly opposed Christians (Acts 6:8–8:3) and had killed their leaders. Believers lived in fear of him.

After Paul realized the truth of the gospel, he turned his life around completely. He was deeply sorry for his former life as a persecutor. But Paul didn't allow his past to stand in the way of his ministry—he fearlessly went forward with his life. We need to remember that Christ forgives us when we make mistakes, just as He did Paul. We need to receive strength and forgiveness, and go on with life, trusting God to help us. In this vein, the words from *Things That Matter Most* are very encouraging:

And even supposing we have made mistakes, and we would dearly like to have the choice again that we might take the other turning, what then? Who is our God? And what are His name and character? Cannot He knit up the raveled bit of work, and in His own infinite gracious way throw ourselves upon His inexhaustible goodness, and say with St. Teresa, "Undertake Thou for me, O Lord"?

It is the very gospel of His grace that He can repair the things that are broken. He can restore the joints of the bruised reed. He can restore the broken heart. He can deal with the broken vow. And if He can do all this, can He not deal with our mistakes? If unknowingly we went astray and took the wrong turning, will not His infinite love correct our mistakes, and make the crooked straight?[*]

God can take terrible situations and turn them around. And finally, sometimes it's best not to judge too quickly. A good decision doesn't mean everything will be rosy from that point forward. Often there will come trouble, and with it temptation to turn back. But what you first thought was a disaster may turn out to be the best after all!

TAKE ACTION!

Think of a decision you're faced with. Now, using the P O P C O R N decision-making guidelines, write down the results of each step as you do it:

P   Pray for wisdom.

O   List the Options.

P   Weigh the Pros.

C   Weigh the Cons.

O   Open your Bible.

R   Get Recommendations.

N   No hurry!

CHAPTER EIGHT

What's Your Game Plan?

T om and Steve were longtime friends. They took several classes together and were members of the same fraternity. The two were talking over lunch in the student union after their return from summer break.

"How does your schedule look this semester?" asked Tom.

"It's a little heavy. I'm taking nineteen hours again." Steve looked tired as he talked. "I'm trying to finish my degree this year. But I don't know if I'll make it; football practice has been taking a lot of my time."

Tom took a bite from his burger. "What do you plan to do after graduation, Steve?"

"I really don't know," Steve replied with a sigh. "I'm hoping to make a pro team."

"Do you think you stand a chance?" Tom asked with interest.

"No, not really," said Steve. "It's a shot in the dark."

Tom was concerned. "What's your plan if you don't make it?"

"Well, I haven't thought much about that. I can keep my same apartment. I hear the car plant may be hiring soon. Maybe I can get a line job." Steve reached for a cracker.

Tom noticed the Bible with Steve's books and changed the subject. "How are things at your church?"

"I enjoy worshipping there but I don't know if I'll continue. I might look around..." He paused. "What about you, Tom? What are your plans?"

"I just signed a contract with a finance company. I'll be working as a loan officer. It doesn't pay much, but there's room to advance."

Steve reached for another cracker. "And what about Anne? Are you two still serious?"

"Haven't you heard? We're engaged! Our wedding will be next month. Anne got a teaching job, and we're looking for a house in Baker Estates. Oh, there's another thing; Campus Crusade for Christ asked me to help lead a student group."

Steve looked envious. "Tom, it sounds like you have a good plan. I wish I had a better idea of what I'm going to do!"

Five years later, Tom was having lunch in a fast food restaurant. He was looking over the menu when the waiter came up. Tom recognized him, and said brightly, "Steve! I haven't seen you in ages!"

Steve looked a little sheepish. "I thought it might be you when you came in."

"Can you sit and talk a minute?" asked Tom. Steve looked around and then slid into the booth next to him.

"How have you been, Tom?"

"Really well, thanks. Anne and I have two kids and enjoy our home. She's a terrific companion. I'm a partner in my company now, and we recently started a prayer breakfast with the employees. It's been exciting to share my faith with them."

Steve was interested. "What else are you doing?"

"I still work with the student group on campus. They really lead it themselves, but I go to help. This is one of the most fun things I've done since we graduated."

Steve began to feel a little more comfortable. "I wish I could say what you've just said. I'm still living in the same apartment. I've been working at odd jobs and haven't been to church in two years." He paused and tilted his head back. "I just never had much direction." Then Steve's eyes lit up. "I never play football without some kind of game plan. Maybe I need a better plan for my life, too? Any chance you could help me with this, Tom?"

Tom was pleased at the prospect. "Sure, Steve. I'll do everything I can. Come to my house tomorrow evening. We can toss a ball, have some supper, and talk about it."

"You've got a deal!"

WHAT'S IN A PLAN?

To win, a football team always creates game plans. We too need to plan out our future, too. A wise person once said, "There are a thousand good causes. But if one divides himself between them all he accomplishes nothing. If you can focus on one and pursue it with all you have, perhaps you can make an impact." This was spoken by one whose life project it was to collect and classify squash seeds. Our mission is to agape love Jesus, others, and ourselves. We need to have a plan!

To help us get started, we can use some simple ideas from the field of management. A goal or plan is a statement of what we intend to do, and it's the result of a decision-making process. Some people plan more than others. But like Steve, most of us need to do better.

Above all, planning helps us organize and focus our energy. Many activities require that several steps be carried out. If you want to get a particular job, your plan could look like this: 1) receive the proper training, 2) write a résumé, 3) make applications, and 4) go for interviews. If you organize your efforts beforehand, you'll be less likely to become misguided and fail.

Can you imagine a construction company building a hotel without a plan to guide the project? Inconceivable! The first part of their plan would be to pour a foundation. Next, they would build the external structure. They'd also try to get the roof on before it rains. Finally, the builders would put in the drywall, fixtures, and carpet. Without a plan, they would waste a tremendous amount of time and energy. For example, if they put in the walls and carpeting before the roof was in place, any rain that came along would ruin them! Like builders, we need to plan our lives so we won't waste our resources and talents.

Governments, universities, and the military also set goals and make plans. They wouldn't succeed without them. Paul often spoke of plans in his letters. In Romans 1:13 we read, "I do not want you to be unaware, brothers, that I planned many times to come to you..." He realized he needed a strategy if he was going to evangelize the world (Acts 19:21; 20:16; Romans 15:28; 1 Corinthians 4:19, 16:5-7).

God is concerned about our plans. Proverbs 16:3 reminds us to "Commit to the LORD whatever you do, and your plans will succeed." Building our plans around our faith demonstrates what we really believe, and helps us to accomplish our goals! James

4:13-17, on the other hand, describes the plight of those who boast of their plans without giving credit to God.

God has plans, too. Concerning the people of ancient Israel, he says in Jeremiah 29:11, " 'For I know the plans I have for you,' declares the LORD, 'plans to prosper you and not to harm you, plans to give you a hope and a future.' " If God is so concerned about his plan for these people, we can't afford to ignore our own plans, either!

PLANNING YOUR BEST GAME!

Good plans result from careful decision-making. Use the POPCORN guidelines introduced in Chapter 7. For example, suppose you are considering starting a business. Before you decide, pray for wisdom, list your options, weigh the pros and cons, open your Bible for advice, get recommendations, and don't be in a hurry. The greater the commitment involved, the more careful you should be. What do good plans look like?

1) *They are realistic.* How much time, money, and energy is required? Do you have the resources? Each of us has definite financial, emotional, physical, and mental limits to consider. Some people always seem to fail because they give themselves formidable tasks to perform that have little chance to succeed. So, take a moment to think. Visualize yourself at work. This will help you to understand the job in front of you and assess whether you actually can do it. The object is not necessarily to make bigger plans, but to make plans that are attainable.

2) *They should be specific.* This way, you will be aiming at a target goal and will know when you hit it. Instead of saying, "I will

make better grades," say, "I will make at least a 'B' average next semester." Rather than make a plan to be more friendly, make a plan to talk with Sarah every week. The best plans are the ones that can be written down, measured, and given a deadline.

3) They may need to be flexible. Occasionally your situation will change. You may also need to change your plans. For example, you might intend to spend a weekend at the lake, but if your father becomes ill you might want to go home instead. Or when a friend is lonely, you may need to cut a class or church service and go spend time with that friend.

Flexibility means we can manage to fulfill our mission in spite of changing circumstances. The Bible includes flexibility in the two concepts of time it describes. The first is *hora* or *chronos*. This refers to the days, hours, and minutes by which we plan or record our activities. The second is *kairos*. It means "event" or "opportunity." We need to be alert to the often unexpected opportunities or circumstances that come up! This is where flexibility comes in. Remember, our lives should not center around plans, but people. We're not following a process but a Person—Jesus Christ.

4) The best plans are JOYful. That is, they will be full of consideration for your relationship with Jesus, Others, and Yourself. Many people become so occupied with one aspect of life—work or school, for example—that they neglect others. This usually is not wise. Instead, we must remember each of our important relationships. Our plan can be a tool to help us do this.

PASS, RUN, OR PUNT?

Shauna was in a hurry. It was eight o'clock at night and she still had a speech to prepare for class the next day. Her books were spread out over the table. Shauna was thinking of the introduction to her speech when her eyes fell upon the calendar on the wall. "Oh, no!" she said, "I almost forgot. I promised to help Maria with her Spanish tomorrow! I'll need to prepare for that, too." She was feeling tired but went back to work.

Suddenly there was a knock at the door. Shauna got up and opened it. Five of her friends were there. "We're going to a movie!" one of them said. "Please come with us!"

Now Shauna was really in a fix. She wanted so badly to have some fun! But there was her speech and the Spanish lesson. She thought about how tired she was. "I'd really like to go," she said, "but I'm swamped. I don't know what to do!"

Like Shauna, sometimes we feel overwhelmed, bombarded, and nearly suffocated by the circumstances and choices we must make. We are pounded with opportunities, assignments, requests, referrals, demands, and threats. But each of us has limited energy and time. Some things must be eliminated! We have to decide which are most important, and to focus our energy on these. Only then can we avoid the inevitable fatigue, inefficiency, depression, frustration, and failure that comes from attempting too much. Some Christians try to resolve this tension by ranking their relationships and saying that God is first, family is second, church is third, and so forth. Then when a conflict comes up between church and work, for example, the church activity automatically wins out.

While there seems to be some wisdom in this approach, it also raises hard questions. For example, what does it mean to put God first? Does it mean we must pray eight hours a day? Should we do *anything* that would put God second? Does it mean that when we study, God is out of the picture and work now comes first? If our witness to nonbelievers is more important than our work, should we even go to work? And finally, if our personal needs are in last place, how can we justify eight hours of sleep, two hours of eating, and fifteen minutes in the shower each day? If the time we allot is the measure, then we certainly are priority number one!

There is a better way. Earlier, we looked at the great commandment found in Matthew, chapter 22:37-40, " 'Love the LORD your God with all your heart and with all your soul and with all your mind.' This is the first and greatest commandment. And the second is like it: 'Love your neighbor as yourself.' All the Law and the Prophets hang on these two commandments."

Now look closely at this passage. How does Jesus classify the second command? He says it is *like* the first one. The word "like," or *homoios* in the original Greek language, is an important one. It means "similar to this." Jesus is indicating that the second command mentioned, to love others as yourself, is also "great and foremost" because it is "like" the first commandment. *It's just as important.* Second in this context does not indicate second in rank, for the two commands are not being ranked, but listed. Victor Paul Furnish, in *The Love Command in the New Testament*, puts it like this: "In effect, then, the scribe is being told that no one command can be marked as 'first,' but that these two together...constitute the essence of the law."[1]

Jesus is reminding us that our mission is to love God, others, and ourselves. When we do this there are tremendous overlapping effects. No relationship is exclusive. J. Grant Howard elaborates on this idea:

> There are three priorities in life. My responsibility to God, to others, and to myself. They are closely related to each other. Let's make that a stronger statement. They are inextricably tied together. When you pray, you are loving God. That's putting God first, but it is also putting yourself first, because you benefit from praying. When you memorize Scripture, you are loving God and in so doing putting Him first. At the same time, you are profiting from the Word and that means you are meeting your own needs, too. When you worship and praise God, He is pleased because of your response to Him. Those very same activities are also having an impact on your personal growth.
>
> In the same way, when we fulfill a biblical obligation to a neighbor, we put our neighbor first. But the good deed also has numerous positive effects on us. In carrying out our biblical responsibilities to God and neighbors, we are always in some way involved. We are always in some way both contributor and receiver.[2]

When we set priorities, our intention is to be faithful within *each* of our important relationships, while staying within the limits of our time and energy. This isn't such a foreign idea. When we live on a budget, we have a certain amount of money to spend. We draw upon this to pay for essentials like food, housing, clothes, utilities, tuition, and books, without overdrawing our account. Likewise, when we set priorities, we decide how to divide our resources to undertake various activities. When confronted with several conflicting possibilities, ask yourself:

- How am I doing in my relationships now? Is there one area that needs more attention?
- How much time and energy do I have? Am I already overcommitted?
- How will this activity affect my relationships in the future? Will it help in an area that needs more attention? Will it detract from a relationship in which I already need to put more effort?
- How much time and energy will this activity take? How often does it need to be done? Some things take little time, yet in the long run may save much time, pain, and expense—like changing oil in the car. Other matters, like being a leader at church or going to college, will take considerable effort no matter what.
- What will be the consequences if I don't do this activity? Will it matter a week, month, or year from now? If nothing bad will happen, then perhaps the task is not so important in the first place. General Eisenhower was right when he said, "The urgent is seldom important, and the important seldom urgent."

The surest way to deal with conflicting priorities is to choose that which will best help us maintain our most important relationships. Say no to the other options! This conviction helped Shauna survive in the above story. She decided her studies, and helping Maria by preparing a Spanish lesson, were more important than watching a movie the night her friends came by. Mature people are those who can see all the options, understand how much energy they have, and then choose what will help them best support their most important relationships.

JUST HOW MUCH IS ENOUGH?

Most of us live under tremendous pressure to do more and more—earn more money, see more friends, serve more people, keep the car more clean. This leads to stress. Of course, not all stress is bad. At times it motivates us to perform when we would not do so otherwise, thus saving us from hazardous situations. However, stress is harmful when it is prolonged and excessive. Most Americans, including young adults, live under damaging stress all the time and suffer the consequences of physical illness, depression, poor school or job performance, disturbed family or dating relations, and so on.

Richard Swenson is a physician whose stressful life parallels that of many of us. He was busy with many good activities—he had a successful professional life, held leadership positions in the church, cared for his wife and children, and ministered to friends. He knew these activities and relationships were important. But Richard also felt a growing sense of frustration and exhaustion— he was nearing burnout.

Then he made a lifestyle change designed to take back control of his life. Richard painstakingly reexamined all of his "good" activities, weighing them in order of importance, paying close attention to his own emotional, spiritual, and financial resources.

And as he cut back, ninety percent of his psychological pain disappeared.

He also made a startling discovery:

> With more time on my hands, I began to examine the forces that were so chaotically propelling not only my schedule but our culture, too. Where was all the stress coming from? Why was there so much anxiety, frustration, and depression? Why were so many people so unhappy even though they had so much?...
>
> It was the pathological absence of what I call "margin"— the gap between rest and exhaustion, the space between breathing freely and suffocating. Margin, the leeway between our reserves and our limits, was missing.... Overload is clearly a common American experience and, naturally, margin is in epidemic short supply. From activity overload to debt overload to work overload, we are a society running on empty....
> I discovered that the vast majority of people are better off if they draw the line somewhere short of overload, if they preserve some margin.[3]

When I was in college, I had a class on Monday nights, taught guitar lessons on Tuesday evenings, had a Fellowship of Christian Athletes meeting on Wednesdays, and a church youth group meeting on Thursday nights. When Fridays came, I was always exhausted!

These were all good activities but I was frustrated and not doing any of them very well. I also was neglecting my own need to study and have periods of rest and relaxation. Something had to go. I desperately needed "margin." It was difficult, but I cut back to going out only two nights a week. I was happier and did a better job with the limited activities I chose. Setting limits, and vigorously sticking to them, helped me to survive college!

Just how much is enough? If you love God, cherish your mate, care for those in your church, share Jesus with nonbelieving friends, do your work well, and take care of your personal needs—this is enough! Before setting out to change the world, our private lives must be in order. Most of us are doing well to accomplish this goal alone.

Our objective in life is not simply to have our schedules filled with activity, nor is it to earn points with God. Rather, our objective is to be *fulfilled* through understanding who we are in Jesus, and expressing that identity by the way we live. Our culture would have us driven by compulsions and threats. Instead, let's stand against these and be drawn forward by the love and security of Jesus.

WHAT'S YOUR GAME PLAN?

In football, the competition is divided into halves and quarters. This gives the teams a chance to rest and plan for the next period of play. Our lives also can be divided into segments, for similar reasons. Parallel with halves and quarters might be school semesters, the days between holidays, the weeks between vacations, four years of high school, four years of college, or three years of an employment contract. In each segment of life, we can form a plan for what we want to accomplish in each of our relationships. This takes time and effort. But the investment is usually rewarded several times over with more successes and fewer frustrations.

A loose-leaf notebook is a useful tool in which to keep your plans organized. First, choose a time segment, like the three months between now and your next significant break from school or work. What do you want to do during this time period? Write it down. Concentrate on what you *most* want to accomplish, and ruthlessly weed out everything else. The idea is not necessarily to do more. Rather, it's to do the best things! Put this list in your notebook. It might look similar to the following one:

PERSONAL PLAN (JANUARY TO MARCH)

Relating to JESUS:

—Pray for understanding of spiritual gifts.

—Read the Gospels.

Relating to OTHERS:

Family:

—Take trips to visit Mom and Dad February 14 and March 25.

—Buy birthday gifts for cousins Jane and Roger.

Believers:

—Visit three potential churches each month.

—Have breakfast with Tom every Tuesday.

Nonbelievers:

—Invite Luke to a prayer breakfast.

—Meet with the Campus Crusade leaders.

People at work:

—Ace the final exam in Spanish.

—Be on time for work every day this month.

The nation:

—Talk to an Air Force recruiter.

—Attend a pro-life rally.

Relating to YOURSELF:

—Run every other day in the mornings.

—Plan my ski trip for December.

Life is interconnected, and we simply can't afford to concentrate on one area at the expense of all others. For this reason, your plans need to be comprehensive, addressing your most important relationships. Look at your plan as *freeing*—freeing you to do what is most essential. Forget the notion that it's restrictive. It's there to serve you—and not the reverse!

When you reach your deadline, look at your list and write "Done!" beside each accomplishment. Congratulate yourself. It feels good! Then, write a plan for the next segment of time. It might look like this:

PERSONAL PLAN (APRIL TO JUNE)

Relating to JESUS:

—Pray for understanding of Jesus' second coming.

—Read Acts, Romans, and Corinthians.

Relating to OTHERS:

Family:

—Go to the family reunion in June.

—Call my cousins each month.

Believers:

—Attend the new members meeting at Southside Church.

—Play basketball with Tom on Saturdays.

Nonbelievers:

—Talk with Luke about how I became a Christian.

—Share about Jesus when I give a presentation at work.

People at work:

—Register for the summer term.

—Develop a new accounting system for the office.

The nation:

—Get advice from an Air Force officer.

—Write my congressmen on the abortion issue.

Relating to YOURSELF:

—Try out for the basketball team.

—Save $50 each month for my ski trip in December.

The length of time your plan covers can vary, depending on your needs. You may have five-year plans, one-year plans, monthly plans, or even plans for a week or a day at a time. Notice how smaller plans can build upon each other to accomplish something larger. For this reason, it sometimes helps to think *backward*. We must first decide which are the greater things we want to accomplish over the long run. Then we can make short-range plans to spell out the objectives we need to accomplish in order to achieve our larger goals.

It's not always easy to be relationship-oriented, nor is it always easy to harness the power of planning. Relationship-oriented people often resist planning, and planners often overlook relationships. For some of us, this new perspective requires quite an adjustment! But if we use our decision-making skills and plan ahead for our relationships, we'll be much more likely to fulfill our mission in life!

TAKE ACTION!

Think about what you want to accomplish in your most important relationships over a certain period of time, like between now and when you graduate. Now, write down your plan:

Relating to JESUS:

Relating to OTHERS:
 Family:

 Believers:

 Nonbelievers:

People at work:

The nation:

Relating to YOURSELF:

CHAPTER NINE

Just Do It!

Our lives are meant to be characterized by love in action. In the book of John, Jesus tells us, "If you love me, you will obey what I command.... Whoever has my commands and obeys them, he is the one who loves me. He who loves me will be loved by my Father, and I too will love him and show myself to him.... If anyone loves me, he will obey my teaching. My Father will love him, and we will come to him and make our home in him" (John 14:15, 21, 23). Jesus is emphasizing here that genuine love can't be separated from action.

You can recognize those who love God by the way they live. True agape love is *love in motion*. We only deceive ourselves if we know what to do but don't follow through: "Suppose a brother or sister is without clothes and daily food. If one of you says to him, 'Go, I wish you well; keep warm and well fed,' but does nothing about his physical needs, what good is it? In the same way, faith by itself, if it is not accompanied by action, is dead" (James 2:15-17).

In *Dropping Your Guard,* Charles Swindoll writes:

When we describe love as a demonstration, it's because there is action, involvement, movement, expression. "Love is...love does. Love is not...love does not." Love doesn't sit back and snooze. It is not apathetic. It is ready and willing. It is neither passive nor indifferent. It refuses to yawn its way through life. Authentic love is demonstrative, not sterile and dull.

I distinctly remember reading about a very interesting case that came before the courts in the state of Massachusetts back in the late 1920s. It concerned a man who had been walking along a pier when suddenly he tripped over a rope and fell into the cold, deep waters of that ocean bay. He came up sputtering, screaming for help, then sank beneath the surface. For some reason he was unable to swim or stay afloat. His friends heard his faint cries in the distance, but they were too far away to rescue him. But within only a few yards was a young man lounging on a deck chair, sunbathing. Not only could the sunbather hear the drowning man plead, "Help, I can't swim," he also was an excellent swimmer. But the tragedy is that he did nothing. He only turned his head to watch indifferently as the man finally sank and drowned.... The opposite of love is apathy, not hatred. Love, sweet love, is a demonstration, not merely an inclination.[1]

Action is the final step to realization. Our allegiance, mission, and specific decisions don't amount to much unless we put them into practice. And as we act upon what we have decided to do, a wonderful thing usually happens: Our allegiance to Jesus, our sense of mission, and our decision-making skills all improve. Our confidence in our ability to handle life begins to blossom. And our experience of inner happiness swells. This positive-feedback cycle can be illustrated like this:

LEADERSHIP → MISSION → PLAN → ACTION

Some simple analogies may help make my point clear. For example, ships are not built to stay in the harbor; they are meant to go to sea. Muscles are not meant to be flabby, but should be flexed and ready for productive work. Christians, too, are meant to set sail and lift weights, and they're *intended to exercise agape love.*

STRENGTH FOR THE WORKOUT

We want to live out our decisions and see our plans through to completion. But this sometimes can be so hard to do! Often opposition, disappointment, illness, temptation, or doubt holds us back or bring a halt to our forward progress altogether: a parent dies; a friend rejects us; we fail a class or lose our job; an argument erupts and splits our church. These things happen to even the most sincere believers. And ultimately, our energy becomes sapped. Where can we possibly get the strength we need to carry on? There are several sources:

• *Strength from God.* When Jesus left the earth he gave us a commission to share the Good News with all the world. But he didn't stop there. He also said, "And surely I will be with you always, to the very end of the age" (Matthew 28:20). Jesus encourages us today through the work of his Spirit in our lives, reminding us of our security in relation to him. Paul wrote about this in his letter to the church at Ephesus: "I pray that out of his glorious riches he may strengthen you with power through his Spirit in your inner being" (Ephesians 3:16).

In 2 Corinthians 1:8-11, we read about some severe problems Paul encountered. He was emotionally drained. He was so depressed that he came close to giving up on living. But in the midst of Paul's despair, God strengthened him. Remember, grace is God's empowering presence, which enables us to be all he created us to be and to do all that he has called us to do! We continually need to receive God's grace for the strength to exercise love. And, we can be secure in the assurance that he will never leave or forsake us (Hebrews 13:5).

• *Strength from others.* We're meant to live as part of a network of believers who share a faith, mission, and Spirit (1 Corinthians 12:12-13). When we live like this, we often have access to a tremendous source of strength. When we make mistakes, someone can gently correct us (James 5:19-20). When we're down emotionally, another can encourage us (Hebrews 10:25). When confronted with a problem, we can put our heads together and find a solution (Acts 6:1-7). Paul, writing in 1 Thessalonians 5:11, tells us, "Therefore encourage one another and build each other up, just as in fact you are doing." Those who live in the midst of loving relationships can respond to challenges with remarkable energy!

I arrived by myself in Shanghai, China, in July 1982, to work at the Third Peoples Hospital. Before leaving the United States, I received the names of some Western Christians who were teaching English in Shanghai. I was looking forward to meeting them. But I soon discovered the teachers were all on vacation. They wouldn't be back until September! I was very disappointed, but slid a note under the door of one teacher, asking him to call me when he returned.

I was having a difficult time adjusting to my new home. My Chinese language skills were poor, causing endless frustration, and people stared at me all the time, having rarely seen a foreigner. Furthermore, Shanghai was a terribly hot and forbidding place in the summer. To top it all off, I was starved for friendship with other Christians. I was thinking seriously about quitting my work in Shanghai and going back to the United States.

Then one day the phone rang. It was the teacher from New Zealand. He'd returned and found my note. He asked if I could meet with him and the others for dinner that night. My response? You guessed it! I was thrilled! For an entire year we met together to pray and talk. Without the encouragement of these Christians I would surely have given up!

• *Strength from inner conviction.* We also can receive strength and encouragement from within if we have a clear conscience and know we're trying to do what's right. Paul referred to this when he said, "Now this is our boast: Our conscience testifies that we have conducted ourselves in the world, and especially in our relations with you, in the holiness and sincerity that are from God" (2 Corinthians 1:12). Inner conviction can especially help when our efforts don't seem to be paying off, or at the times when other people don't understand or support us. Even if we seem to have failed, we can still find joy in our conviction that we have been fighting for the right cause. After all, the truth of our wholeness and security is not ultimately based upon our performance or successes, as we discussed in Chapter 3. Rather, it is based on who we are in Jesus Christ. He gives us L I F E—Love, Inspiration, Forgiveness, and Eternity. These cannot be earned through our activities. They are simply received by believing in Jesus. In this truth we can have hope, peace, and assurance when life gets tough.

READY, SET, GO!

When I was in high school, I read the books of Tom Dooley, a Navy physician from St. Louis. He ran a refugee camp for Vietnamese who had escaped the Communist-controlled part of their country. And as a Christian, he was moved by the tremendous suffering he witnessed. Dr. Dooley found remarkable joy and inspiration in his work, and spent the remainder of his life helping the poor in Southeast Asia.

As I read of his adventures, I was convinced to follow his example. After I finished the years of medical training, I married a lady with similar dreams, and we found an organization willing to send us overseas. Still, I felt as if something were lacking. One evening I shared my hesitation with my mother. She listened intently and then took my hand. "Honey," she said, "you're ready. Now just do it!"

One afternoon a year later, I was on my way to work at the hospital in Kalukembe, Angola. As I drove up in the Land Rover, a nurse from the emergency room stopped me. I recognized him. It was Anthony. "We have a man who just arrived from the bush. His foot was blown off by a land mine. Could you come and see him?"

The man was unconscious, having lost much blood. He was very old. I looked at his chart and saw that his name was John the Baptist. His right leg was wrapped in a gunny sack which was stained dark red. I dreaded removing the sack. We began to give the man intravenous fluids and blood, and took him to the oper-ating room.

Soon, a nurse was giving him a spinal anesthesia. But it didn't make much difference, because he was already unconscious. I was worried that John might have suffered brain damage from the blood loss. When we unwrapped the leg, the bare tibia bone, now stripped of muscle and skin, was jabbing out where the leg had been. The foot was completely gone. The shredded muscles close to the knee draped over the upper leg in an ugly mass. The flesh stank horribly, for the wound was two days old. I turned my head away for a moment to fight off my nausea.

"How did he get here?" I asked.

"He was carried on some poles to a road, and then brought here by car," Anthony replied. "There are several men outside who brought him in."

"How long did it take them?"

"Only about six hours. But you see, this man was not discov-ered until this morning. His sons found him lying in a field."

I shook my head. "Let's pray for him," I said.

All the nurses stopped what they were doing, and I put my hand on the old man's head. "Lord," I said, "we're sad that such a terrible thing has happened to John. We know that you love him. So please help us care for him. Please help him recover. And give us the strength we need, too. We are here because of you, and depend on you to keep us safe."

As I finished speaking, Anthony handed me the disinfectant to cleanse the leg. I scrubbed off the dirt as best I could and drew a line around the upper leg where I would amputate it. Then I wrapped the mangled lower leg in a sterile sheet to keep it from contaminating the rest of the leg's tissues. As I worked, I kept an eye on the blood transfusion dripping into his vein; this is what John needed most, but it seemed to run so slowly! After half an hour I was finished, and we moved him to the intensive care ward. I wrote his medications on his chart and then talked them over with the nurse on duty. As I left, I stopped at his bedside again. John hadn't opened his eyes or moved at all. I thought he'd probably die, and that what we had done had been in vain.

Finally, I went home and found that my family had waited to have supper with me. As I entered the room, Elizabeth, my daughter, shouted and ran to me. Her excitement at my arrival encouraged me. I told my family about my afternoon. I was emotionally and physically drained.

We had just finished eating when there was a knock at the door; it was Anthony again. A child was having an asthma attack and needed help. I examined the girl moments later in the intensive care ward. She was wheezing badly. We gave her some adrenaline. After a few minutes she came around, so we gave her some long-acting medicine to keep her from a relapse.

As I was leaving, I asked the nurse about the old man. He replied, "Why don't you go talk with him?" I was startled, but when I arrived at the man's bedside, he was awake.

John the Baptist was looking right at me. "Well, you must be the doctor," he said. "You helped save my life."

"I'm so glad to see you are awake. I was really worried about you!" I exclaimed.

"I was pretty worried, too," he replied weakly. "I was walking with a sack of seed corn, and the next thing I knew, I was blasted into the air. When I hit the ground, I was afraid to look. The blood was flowing out of my leg in torrents. I was so scared, I could hardly move. But I knew I had to do something." His voice was still feeble, but I could understand his words. "I took off my shirt and tied it tight around my leg. I cried out for help but no one came. As the shock wore off, the pain became excruciating. Then when night fell, I was sure I would never see the morning again. But, as you see, here I am!"

As the weeks wore on, John gradually became better. His leg was healing slowly, and his family brought food to him. He began to gain some weight, and to walk with crutches. After two months he was discharged. Later he could have an artificial leg made. John went back to his village and his plot of land.

Several months later, I had almost forgotten about the episode with John. We were busy with work and chasing after James, our one-year-old. One day I was leafing through the mail. A letter was posted from within the country. *This is strange*, I thought. *I usually only get mail from America.* I opened the envelope. It was from John the Baptist! It read, "Doctor Nicholas, I know that the work of a doctor is difficult. You see so many people and do not have much time for yourself. You do not receive much thanks for what you do. But this is the greatest reward that a doctor can receive, to be thanked by his patient. You have been very kind to me and I will never forget you. Thank you for coming to Angola."

I was so overcome with joy that I dropped the letter. At that moment I knew in my heart that all the struggle to decide what to do with my life, and the years of training and preparation, had been worthwhile. I, too, was glad I had come!

TAKE ACTION!

1)   Think of something important you decided to do but have never actually begun. What can you do to help you take that final step?

2)   Think of a situation in which you had difficulty following through with a decision but were strengthened so that you finally were able to do it. How did this come about? How might you have been strengthened even more?

What Shall I Do with My Life?

Each of us must decide how to live, including choices of marriage, career, church, friends, and neighborhood. The quality of our lives depends much upon these choices. But good decisions usually don't just happen—they more often follow a struggle. What can we do to make better decisions?

OUR LEADER: JESUS CHRIST

We must begin by realizing that many different people may influence our choices: friends, parents, professors, and members of the media, among others. But our best influence is Jesus Christ. He said, "I have come that they may have life, and have it to the full" (John 10:10). Our greatest need is for the security and leadership of Jesus. Our greatest decision is to accept these gifts (John 11:26). This is not simply a one-time choice. Rather, it's a lifestyle in which we continue to believe, day after day.

What does Jesus want us to do? Some people constantly search for specific signs. Though he may supernaturally reveal an individual direction, God usually gives us the privilege and responsibility to choose for ourselves, using the principles and instructions found in the Bible.

OUR MISSION: TO LOVE JESUS, OTHERS, AND SELF

Our *mission* is our highest objective. People choose many different missions or purposes for which to live, including position, possessions, pleasure, and projects. But Jesus explains that our primary purpose as Christians is to love people with agape love—that tough, enduring, committed kind of love. This purpose is to be the theme for our lives (Matthew 22:35-40).

We agape love through building JOYful relationships. That is, relationships with Jesus, Others (including family, believers, nonbelievers, those at work, and our nation), and Yourself. But this often isn't easy. Over time, we need to learn how to do this better (Philippians 1:9-10).

OUR STRATEGY: BUILT WITH WISDOM

Once we know our mission, we can make individual choices concerning how we'll fulfill it (Ephesians 5:15-16). But even in this we're not alone. God offers us wisdom—the ability to assess a situation and determine the best course of action.

The Bible contains much teaching on how to make wise decisions. Many of these points can be summed up in the mnemonic POPCORN:

POPCORN GUIDELINES
FOR DECISION-MAKING

P	Pray for wisdom.
O	List the Options.
P	Weigh the Pros.
C	Weigh the Cons.
O	Open your Bible.
R	Get Recommendations.
N	No hurry!

In every stage of life, we can look at our most important relationships, use the P O P C O R N strategy, and formulate a plan for what we want to accomplish. This will help us focus our energies and keep our attention on people. And finally, we want to follow through with action, doing the things we planned—thus fulfilling our life mission (John 14:15).

Ultimately, our journey through life will take us to a new world. This will be a wonderful place, the marvels of which we can hardly begin to imagine! Revelation 21:3-5 tells us: " 'Now the dwelling of God is with men, and he [God] will live with them. They will be his people, and God himself will be with them and be their God. He will wipe every tear from their eyes. There will be no more death or mourning or crying or pain, for the old order of things has passed away.' He who was seated on the throne said, 'I am making everything new!' "

See you there!

Chapter 1. We Must Decide!

1. J. Grant Howard, *Balancing Life's Demands* (Portland, Oregon: Multnomah Press, 1983), 13-14.

2. *Bridge Over the River Kwai*, Columbia Pictures, 1957.

Chapter 3. Whom Will You Follow?

1. Bobby Richardson Day. A tract published by the American Tract Society (Oradell, New Jersey: 1972).

Chapter 4. How Does God Lead Us?

1. Bruce K. Waltke, "Dogmatic theology and relative knowledge," *CRUX*, Vol. 15, No. 1, (March 1979), 15-18.

2. Gary Friesen with J. Robin Maxson, *Decision Making and the Will of God: A Biblical Alternative to the Traditional View* (Portland, Oregon: Multnomah Press, 1980).

3. Ibid., 187.

Chapter 5. The 5 P's

1. John Boykin, *The Gospel of Circumstance* (Grand Rapids, Michigan: Zondervan, 1991), 153.

2. Klans Bockmuel, *The Challenge of Marxism* (Downers Grove, Illinois: InterVarsity Press, 1983), 129.

3. James Dobson, *What Wives Wish Their Husbands Knew about Women* (Wheaton, Illinois: Tyndale House, 1975), 108.

Chapter 6. Agape Love: Currency of the Kingdom

1. *Webster's New World Dictionary of the American Language* (New York, New York: The Southwestern Company, 1971 edition).

2. J. Grant Howard, *Balancing Life's Demands* (Portland, Oregon: Multnomah Press, 1983).

3. James Dobson, *Dr. Dobson Answers Your Questions* (Wheaton, Illinois: Tyndale House Publishers, 1984), 310-11.

4. Dick Couey, *Happiness Is Being a Physically Fit Christian* (Nashville, Tenn.: Broadman Press, 1985).

Chapter 7. POPCORN Decisions

1. *Webster's New World Dictionary of the American Language* (New York, New York: The Southwestern Company, 1971 edition).

2. J.I. Packer, *Knowing God* (Downers Grove, Illinois: InterVarsity Press, 1973), 80.

3. Spencer Johnson, *The One Minute Manager* (New York, New York: HarperCollins, 1981).

4. John Henry Jowett, *Things That Matter Most* (New York, New York: F. H. Revell, 1913), 206.

Chapter 8. What's Your Game Plan?

1. Victor Paul Furnish, *The Love Command in the New Testament* (Nashville: Abingdon Press, 1972), 27.

2. J. Grant Howard, *Balancing Life's Demands* (Portland, Oregon: Multnomah Press, 1983), 45-46.

3. Richard Swenson, "Overcoming Overload," in *Physician*, (Focus on the Family, January/February 1994), 20.

Chapter 9. Just Do It!

1. Charles Swindoll, *Dropping Your Guard* (Waco, Texas: Word Publishers, 1983), 121.